ATER
Q

Mindy Merrell
&
R. B. Quinn

BROADWAY BOOKS · NEW YORK

BROADWAY

PUBLISHED BY BROADWAY BOOKS

Published in the United States by Broadway Books,
an imprint of The Doubleday Publishing Group,
a division of Random House, Inc., New York.
www.broadwaybooks.com

BROADWAY BOOKS and its logo, a letter B bisected on the
diagonal, are trademarks of Random House, Inc.

Book design by Elizabeth Rendfleisch

Library of Congress Cataloging-in-Publication Data
Merrell, Mindy.
Cheater BBQ / by Mindy Merrell and R.B. Quinn. —1st ed.
    p. cm.
1. Barbecue cookery. I. Quinn, R. B. II. Title.

TX840.B3M47 2008
641.7'6—dc22
                        2008009476

ISBN 978-0-7679-2768-0

PRINTED IN THE UNITED STATES OF AMERICA

10 9 8 7 6 5 4 3 2 1

First Edition

·······CONTENTS·······

Introduction

*C*heater BBQ is about the freedom to make your own barbecue—indoors or out, at home, at the lake, in the parking lot, on the road, even in a studio apartment, no matter the weather. If you've got a slow cooker or an oven, a roll of aluminum foil, some all-natural bottled smoke, and some time, you can have terrific barbecued ribs, chicken, pulled pork, and brisket *and* get a good night's sleep, spend a full day at work, or have plenty of time to relax and follow the game or the race.

Think about that while we tell you our story.

We are a couple who live in Nashville, Tennessee, with two separate homes and busy lives. Min has two children and a dog in the suburbs. R. B. lives in the city with a cat and a patio cluttered with smokers and grills. Together we cook and write about food.

R. B. is one of those guys with an acute case of obsessive barbecue syndrome. His idea of fun is puttering on the patio, splitting hickory and oak, mixing dry rubs by the pound, brining and basting large meat cuts, and micromanaging coals and vents for hours. He even built a two-ton smoker out of a steel smokestack from a nineteenth-century New England textile mill.

Min is a land-grant university home ec major who has been cooking, writing, and developing recipes for more than twenty years. She putters in her well-stocked home test kitchen that never seems to close, and her favorite recipe is the one she hasn't tried yet. The kids never know what "experimental dinner night" has in store for them. Open her refrigerator and a tub of something falls on your foot.

Back in 2004, when R. B. was trolling for weekly grilling column material, he persuaded Min to enter a barbecue competition with him. The two of us had judged plenty of events as Kansas City Barbecue Society judges, mostly the Jack Daniel's Invitational, but had never put R. B.'s own barbecue to the test. We packed the truck with a couple of worn-out bullet smokers, two folding chairs and a table, a pop-up canopy, grilling gear, and coolers and headed east to Cookeville, Tennessee. Surrounded by giant smoking rigs and RVs, we called ourselves "The Carolina Rhodies" after R. B.'s hometown and set up our modest little camp in the parking lot behind the town square. All night, R. B. poked the smokers while Min dozed in the truck.

After the longest night of all time, we turned in our entries on schedule. Min styled our competition Styrofoam clamshells with regulation leaf lettuce and gorgeous slices of beef brisket, a lovely pile of pulled pork with just the right amount of sauce and crusty reddish-black burnt ends, perfectly glazed baby back ribs, and tight-skinned golden brown chicken thighs worthy of a photo shoot. It was our first competition, but we were feeling pretty good about our chances.

We didn't come close to winning. In fact, we came in next to last.

And we had a ball. Just taking in the carnival scene, meeting people we wouldn't have met otherwise, hanging out on our makeshift patio in a parking lot all night, we were a part of the whole barbecue myth and mystique in full swing. Winning something would have been nice, but we came away with something better. We figured out that barbecue in the real world isn't about trophies, score sheets, and matching shirts. It's about cooking good food and feeding people. It's about relaxing and having a good time.

But are any of us having a good time? And are we making any barbecue at home? Or have the television pit masters and celebrity chef bar-b-gurus got us a little intimidated? Somewhere amidst the rules-bound competitive barbecue circuit and extravagant stainless steel outdoor kitchens, are we losing sight of cooking and eating and laughing and talking?

Don't get us wrong, outdoor smoking and grilling is a blast. R. B. can go on for hours about this or that epic moment in his own barbecue history. But outdoor barbecue is also the kind of fun that's hard to enjoy in everyday life. What about the other 359 days of the year? What, no barbecue?

Sure you can have barbecue. That's why we wrote this book. We've combined R. B.'s weekend outdoor expertise and Min's weeknight kitchen sense to create barbecue recipes for any situation. Once we gave ourselves permission to make cheater barbecue in the kitchen without feeling like sellouts, we found ourselves with a lot more choices. We're using the same low and slow barbecue techniques and getting our smoke from a bottle.

That's all we're offering with *Cheater BBQ*—the freedom to choose. You decide whether to soak wood chips and start a fire or open a bottle of smoke and a beer. Or, do some of both. You decide to make barbecue on your own terms, according to your lifestyle, your cooking skills, your equipment, and the weather.

Everyone needs choices. Sometimes outdoor barbecue isn't possible, practical, or even your kind of thing. With *Cheater BBQ*, you decide.

KITCHEN CHEAT SHEET

SLOW COOKERS AND OVENS

Ovens and slow cookers are barbecue-ready with the turn of a knob. Think of them as barbecue pits without the fire, delivering steady, low heat without tinkering or trouble. The slow cooker's heating coil wraps around the thick stoneware insert like an electric blanket, with no danger of burning foods. In your oven, set a low temperature and seal in moisture and smoke by wrapping foods in foil or covering the roasting pan.

Just like outdoor smoking, if you're looking, you ain't cooking. Keep the slow cooker lid shut and the oven door closed and resist the temptation to poke around the meat. Low-temperature cooking takes time for the heat to build up and to regain lost heat. With barbecue, there's really no need to check the meat until near the end of cooking. Unlike a steak or a cake, barbecue isn't ready at a critical moment. An hour here or there isn't going to ruin anything. Even after you decide it's done, the meat can stay put at a low temperature.

The difference between low and high on a slow cooker is more about timing than temperature. Both the low and high settings work fine for cooking anything. Low just takes longer. Typical barbecue meat cuts require 8 to 10 hours on low and 4 to 6 hours on high.

Ovens are easy to set and forget. Optimal barbecue cooking temperatures range from 250°F to 325°F. Many outdoor barbecue guys don't want the fire to get above 275°F. Some stay as low as 225°F, taking a longer cooking time. Pick your favorite temperature setting according to your schedule. It's all good and it all works.

In most of the ultimate cheater meat recipes, we often don't add any liquid to the pot other than bottled smoke. Meat swimming in too much added liquid just stews and can't develop a barbecue crust. We've found that well-marbled meats have plenty of fat and retain plenty of moisture in a sealed pot or under foil. You'll be surprised how much liquid will be in the pot after cooking a pork butt or even a brisket.

Since we're crazy about leftovers, we tend toward large cuts of meat, so the 5- to 7-quart oval slow cooker models are the most useful. We can easily fit a 7- to 9-pound pork butt or a couple of cut-up racks of ribs in our big models. However, the medium crocks (4 quarts) are ideal for smaller roasts, fewer chicken pieces, or a pot of beans.

You can buy the Chevy model slow cooker or the Porsche. Same goes for the oven. Stainless steel doesn't make a bit of difference in anything but kitchen decor. They all get you there and produce excellent cheater barbecue.

DRY RUB CONTAINERS A bunch of glass jars with tight-fitting lids make dry rub prep and storage a cinch. Get different sizes so you can mix up as much of a particular rub as you like. Canning jars work great. Stored in your spice cabinet, dry rubs will last at least a year. They make nice hostess gifts as well.

RIMMED BAKING SHEETS Min's kitchen workhorses are two heavy-duty 12 x 17-inch rimmed metal baking sheets. We use them for just about everything. Unlike a flat cookie sheet, the pan has a one-inch rim to catch meat juices when roasting and barbecuing. Min's are beat up and work fabulously. Spring for good ones.

HEAVY-DUTY ALUMINUM FOIL Thicker, wider foil is best for wrapping heavy meats, especially for oven packets and hobo crock cooking.

DISPOSABLE ALUMINUM PANS We can't exist without a stack of 10 x 12-inch food-service steam table foil pans from the big box stores. Use them for traveling with barbecue and for cooking vegetable packets indoors or even on the grill. Reuse them, then recycle when they're shot.

SEALABLE PLASTIC BAGS Get quart-size freezer bags for leftovers. Anything bigger takes way too long to thaw. One- and two-gallon storage bags are perfect for marinades and brines.

KOSHER SALT If you've yet to make the switch in the kitchen from regular iodized salt to this "gourmet" favorite for its clean salt flavor and flaky texture, now's the time. We call for and have tested all our recipes using kosher salt. If you're using regular salt, you may not need quite as much in these recipes. A box looks like it will last forever, but will be gone before you know it, especially when you get into making your own dry rubs.

CUTTING BOARDS AND SHARP CARVING AND CHOPPING KNIVES Drop your knives off for sharpening or use a stone or steel to maintain a safe edge. Boards need to be bigger than a sheet of paper to handle large cuts of meat and racks of ribs. We like boards that are about 12 x 18 inches. A larger board is okay, but harder to wash because it won't fit into our (or most) kitchen sinks.

TONGS Barbecue absolutely requires sturdy, spring-loaded locking tongs, whether you're cooking indoors or outdoors. Don't bother with cheap, flexible tongs or the really long ones that come in grilling kits. R. B. uses his 9-inch tongs all the time. Much longer than 12 inches and they're cumbersome, tiring, and hard to store.

MEAT THERMOMETERS Instant-read thermometers take the guesswork out of cooking meat. Replace them periodically because they wear out from getting banged around in the drawer. We start each year with a couple of new ones and prefer the dial style that doesn't require batteries.

FREEZER TAPE AND PERMANENT MARKERS Keep track of cooked foods and manage leftovers with easy-to-remove kitchen masking tape and good permanent markers for identifying and dating all leftovers. Leave the tape and markers in the front of your most opened kitchen drawer. Time passes, freezer burn sets in, memories fade. Happens to all of us.

SMOKE CHEAT SHEET

LIQUID SMOKE

Relax, open your mind, and read.

Liquid smoke is exactly that—smoke from smoldering hardwoods or fruitwoods, condensed in water with impurities and carcinogens removed. It is not chemical or synthetic. It is safe, consistent, time-saving, economical, and environmentally friendly smoke in a bottle.

Liquid smoke is a cheater BBQ essential—a critical ingredient for making great barbecue without a fire. We know that it gets a bad rap, but after a year of testing, we still don't understand its undeserved reputation as some kind of imposter. Maybe it's all in the name. Ironically, scores of products boast "natural smoke flavor"; they just leave off the "liquid" part. That said, it's time liquid smoke got a new name and a fresh start.

We call it bottled smoke. It tastes and smells like real smoke because it *is* real smoke. It has been accepted by the U.S. Food and Drug Administration since the early 1960s. Just like traditional wood smoke, not only does bottled smoke deliver great flavor, it also still performs the age-old job of inhibiting spoilage and reducing pathogens in meats. Bottled smoke filters out the eye-burning and cough-inducing carcinogens generated during traditional wood burning. Like using a nicotine patch or gum, you get the buzz (the flavor) without the damaging effects of the tars from airborne smoke.

Consistency is the biggest challenge in outdoor barbecue. The weather, the wind, the wood, the temperature, the equipment, the time, the rub, the mop, the meat, the mood—everything is a determining factor in the outcome of barbecue. And that's a big part of the fun. Bottled smoke paired with the controlled environment of the indoor kitchen eliminates more than half of these iffy variables. That's fun, too.

Bottled Smoke in the Store

The modern appetite for smoke-flavored foods is insatiable. Food manufacturers, the foodservice industry, and home cooks use millions of gallons and pounds of natural smoke flavoring every year. Take a walk down any grocery aisle and you'll see dozens of products listing "natural smoke flavor" as an ingredient—even in things that don't claim to be smoky, like "hearth" pizza crust.

Colgin, the largest U.S. producer of retail bottled smoke, is the brand we see most often in our area. Their product is a dark blend of water, smoke flavor, vinegar, and molasses. Hickory and mesquite are the bestselling flavors, but Colgin has also introduced pecan- and apple-flavored bottled smoke. Other smoke blends we find on the shelf are made by Reese and Figaro. Both include sugar and other ingredients to temper the smoke.

Wright's Concentrated Liquid Smoke, another popular brand, is a little different. It is a concentrate of natural hickory or mesquite smoke blended with only water. It is lighter in color and highly smoke flavored without the marinade-style sweet and sour notes. Lazy Kettle is a small brand that is also a smoke concentrate.

Retail bottled smoke is usually shelved near the barbecue sauces, ketchup, and marinades in supermarkets, natural food stores, specialty and gourmet shops, and online stores. It is most often sold in $3^1/2$- to 5-ounce bottles. One small bottle is generally enough for one good-size pork butt or brisket, or a three-pack of ribs. Bottled smoke can also be dashed into dishes a little at a time like hot pepper sauce. Be prepared for both uses by stocking the pantry. If you're committing to indoor barbecue, you'll need a stash. Larger bottles of some brands, like gallons of Colgin and quarts of Wright's, can be ordered easily over the Internet. Don't worry about it going bad; bottled smoke doesn't need refrigeration and enjoys a long shelf life.

How Much Smoke Is Just Right?

Now there's the barbecue question of all time—one with no real answer, whether you are smoking over a wood fire or indoors in the oven. It's like asking who makes the best barbecue or sauce. It's up to you. The better question is, How much is too much? With smoke, you know it when you taste it. We've had plenty of bitter, chemical-tasting, oversmoked outdoor barbecue. However, we've never had oversmoked, chemical-tasting indoor barbecue. One reason may be that bottled smoke is infinitely easier to measure and manage consistently than wood chunks and charcoal. All the brands are a little different, so you'll have to do some testing on your own.

Colgin recommends one teaspoon per serving as a good starting point. With a concentrate like Wright's, we sometimes use less because of the more concentrated flavor. As a general rule of thumb, for the marinade blends like Colgin, we start with about one tablespoon of bottled smoke per pound of meat. This amount has never smoked us out and is actually quite conservative. We've also used Wright's at this level, producing recipes with a more smoky profile. No matter how much you like to use, bottled smoke manufacturers say the flavor does not diminish during cooking and can be added at any point during cooking. Like lots of flavors and seasonings, smoke should be added to suit your taste. The only way to find that out is to get in the kitchen and get cooking.

Where There's Smoke, There's a Party

The mere smell of smoke sets the inviting party mood of a barbecue. If half the enjoyment of eating is aroma, then bottled smoke will have your guests salivating by the time they say "hello." Bottled smoke provides as much smoky aroma as outdoor wood smoke and will convert your kitchen into a barbecue pit. In all of our recipe testing, every visitor to our kitchens—the plumber, the UPS guy, the neighbors, the oven repairman—reacted the same way. "Y'all cooking barbecue?" That was a good sign.

Use Bottled Smoke Outdoors

Bottled smoke works just as well outdoors. We've met plenty of barbecue fans who regularly add bottled smoke to brines, marinades, basting mops, and sauces for foods that are cooked over real wood fires, charcoal, and gas. The efficient and popular gas grill is particularly in need of a little wood smoke flavor. Wright's even recommends "smoke on the rocks," flavoring your gas grill's lava rocks with their smoke.

Try Bottled Smoke Beyond Barbecue

We've had lots of luck adding bottled smoke to many foods beyond the usual barbecue meats and seafood, including vegetables, fruits, and even beer and chocolate. Anything that tastes great on a grill tastes great with a little smoke. Desserts featuring brown sugar, nuts, any caramel character, or chocolate are particularly suited for smoke.

OTHER KINDS OF SMOKE

SMOKED PAPRIKA Unlike regular spice rack paprika, used mainly to add a nice rusty color to deviled eggs and to our cheater dry rubs, Spanish smoked paprika is a different flavor story altogether.

Spanish smoked paprika, called pimentón de la Vera, is made from peppers slowly dried over oak fire, resulting in a deep earthy taste. Smoked paprika comes in three styles: *dulce* (sweet), *agridulce* (bittersweet), and *picante* (hot). Because of its pungent flavor and varying heat levels, you'll need to experiment with how much you like in a recipe.

We've found that the stuff can be quite addicting. Min's been sneaking spoonfuls into all kinds of dishes like vinaigrette and mayonnaise, and blending it with oil or butter for steaks and fish. Try sprinkling some on any potato dish and on vegetables. It's a must in paella and is the key seasoning in Spanish chorizo. We even like it dusted along with salt on melon. You can also add some to our cheater rubs, replacing some of the regular paprika. We've seen smoked paprika in the lineup of at least one common grocery store brand. It's fine, but not as rich in flavor as the fancy Spanish tins we've bought online (www.thespicehouse.com, www.latienda.com).

CHIPOTLE PEPPERS These days the smoke flavor of chipotle peppers seems as common as the nearest fast-food joint. Chipotles are smoked jalapeño peppers, offering a two-for-one deal on spicy heat and smoke. They are available dried whole and, as with all dried peppers, we soak them in warm water and blend the softened peppers into a paste to use in recipes. Chipotle chile powder is also readily available for sprinkling smoky heat into dishes.

Canned chipotles in adobo sauce (a spicy tomato-ish gravy) are probably the most common chipotle product. We just don't understand why we can't find them packed in resealable jars. It's unusual to use a whole can at once, so freeze the rest in small portions in sealable plastic bags.

SMOKED SALTS We've learned a lot about smoke flavor from Nashville's Radius 10 restaurant, where chef/owner Jason Brumm and chef de cuisine Chad Combs, a Tennessee boy from Cookeville, are always on the lookout for ways to cleverly incorporate country smoke into their big-city food. For a while, the restaurant's dessert menu included Campfire Brownies served on a plate and under a small glass bowl, swirling in smoke from a smoldering hickory chip.

These two curious cooks offered us our first taste of coarse hickory-smoked sea salt. When we placed a few of the exotic dark gray pebbles on our tongues, POW, the flavor exploded in our mouths like smokehouse country ham.

Chad is an avid outdoor smoker, but also a restaurant cheater who appreciates the power of smoked salt's ability to add depth to a dish. He makes his own cheater dry rub for racks of oven ribs, using dozens of seasonings along with smoked salt and smoked paprika.

Fancy smoked salts are a nice little indulgence in the kitchen for adding sophisticated smokiness. A quick Internet search and you'll find sea salts from Maine to France smoked over all varieties of woods (www.saltworks.us). They are best as a finishing touch, a few flavor-packed grains sprinkled over a dish. One thing is for sure, smoked salts get everyone's attention and get everyone talking.

CHAPTER 1

Cheater Beginnings

Oven-Smoked Almonds

Cortez Salsa

Deviled Egg Spread with Smoked Paprika

Smoky Pecan Cheese Ball

Smoked Paprika Pimiento Cheese

Cheater Foie Gras

Hot Peño Noir Spinach Cheese Dip

Any Smoked Fish Party Spread

Cheesy Alligator Snouts

Roasted Eggplant White Bean Spread

Hot-Oven Garlic Heads

Hot-Oven Drums

Rooster Riblets

Quick Sticks

Broiled Kielbasa and Pineapple Picks

Cheata Rita Pitcher

Sparkling Sangria

Hazy Mary

Sparkling Shandy

Red Zingria

Cheater Hot Cider

Eye-Patch Punch

Oven-Smoked Almonds

*L*ike popcorn, nuts taste best sprinkled with extra-fine-grained salt that sticks to the snack. That's why the cheater thing to use here is Lawry's seasoned salt, a ready-to-go finely ground blend of salt, seasonings, and sugar that becomes one with the nut. If you use coarse kosher salt, you'll find the flakes sitting in the bottom of the bowl. You can smoke all kinds of nuts—peanuts, pecans, whatever you like—but the nuts must be raw. Stay close to the oven during the final ten minutes of roasting. The toasty fragrance will let you know when they are ready.

MAKES 2 CUPS

2 cups raw almonds

1 tablespoon peanut or olive oil

1 tablespoon bottled smoke

1 teaspoon fine-grained seasoned salt (we use Lawry's)

Pinch of cayenne pepper

HEAT the oven to 300°F.

COMBINE all the ingredients in a 9 x 13-inch baking pan or on a rimmed baking sheet. Toss until the nuts are well coated with the oil and seasonings. Spread the nuts in a single layer.

BAKE for 25 to 30 minutes, until the nuts are fragrant and toasted.

COOL the nuts and store them in a tightly covered container.

Cortez Salsa

For more than fifty years, Min's two family branches, the Merrells and the Almys, have been eating at the Cortez Cafe in Carlsbad, New Mexico. The food is straightforward Tex-Mex and always finishes with a round of sopapillas and honey.

Back in the '70s, the family thought nothing odd about beginning meals with bowls of fiery green salsa scooped up with saltine crackers. The Cortez has since switched to tortilla chips and you may prefer them as well, but the Merrell-Almy clan retains its hot spot for salsa and crackers.

Pining away in Nashville for that distinct Cortez flavor, Min thinks she's figured it out—it's mostly fresh jalapeños. Min's cousin Eric, knighted Sir Cortez by the clan, now brings his version of Min's Cortez Salsa recipe to every family dinner—with sleeves of only the freshest saltines, of course.

MAKES ABOUT 3 CUPS

15 fresh jalapeño peppers, stems removed, cut in half (we leave the seeds in)

1 medium onion, quartered

One 14$\frac{1}{2}$-ounce can diced tomatoes

1 garlic clove

Juice of 1 lime

Kosher salt to taste

Saltine crackers or tortilla chips

PLACE all the ingredients except the crackers in the bowl of a food processor.

PULSE until the texture is an even, slightly chunky puree. Serve with saltines or chips.

Roasted Jalapeño Salsa

This variation on Cortez Salsa enjoys the added smoky flavor of charred jalapeños and fresh cilantro.

HEAT the broiler. Place the jalapeño peppers on a baking sheet and broil about 4 inches from the heat source until well blistered with patches of charred skin, turning occasionally, about 10 minutes. Proceed with the recipe above, adding a handful of fresh cilantro (large stems removed) to the ingredients.

CHEATER BEGINNINGS

Deviled Egg Spread with Smoked Paprika

Deviled eggs can create a fair amount of anxiety. It's the peeling that's the problem. Experts say older eggs with more of an air pocket peel more easily, some say leave the cooked eggs in the fridge a couple of days before peeling, some say add a little vinegar to the boiling water. All we know is that when it counts, they don't peel.

Deviled Egg Spread with Smoked Paprika is the happy outcome after a fit of frustration with a bowl of broken hard-cooked eggs. Hey, you're thinking, that's just egg salad. So what! The smoked paprika adds the devil and makes a perfectly lovely spread for party rye or crackers.

MAKES 1 1/2 CUPS

6 hard-cooked eggs, finely chopped

1/4 cup mayonnaise

1 tablespoon Dijon mustard

1 teaspoon smoked paprika, plus more for garnish

Hot pepper sauce

Kosher salt and black pepper

Sliced green onions or chives

Crackers, party rye, toasted bagels, or bagel chips

COMBINE the eggs, mayonnaise, mustard, paprika, and hot pepper sauce, salt, and pepper to taste in a medium bowl. Blend well.

SPRINKLE with additional smoked paprika and green onions. Serve with crackers, party rye, toasted bagels, or bagel chips.

Smoky Pecan Cheese Ball

*A*ny appetizer spread, even this one of conventional cheese ball ingredients smashed into a spread, becomes much more glamorous when paired with all things pale green—celery sticks, thin green apple wedges, or Belgian endive. Don't underestimate the allure of a generous pile of green grapes, either.

COMBINE the cheese, pecans, mayonnaise, bottled smoke, and mustard in a medium bowl. Blend well with a fork, adding more mayonnaise if you want a softer, more moist consistency.

ADD the Worcestershire sauce, hot pepper sauce, and pepper to taste and mix well. Sprinkle with paprika. Pile the cheese into a crock and serve with crackers or vegetables and fruit (see head-note).

MAKES ABOUT 2 CUPS

8 ounces sharp Cheddar
    cheese, shredded (2 cups)
$1/2$ cup pecans, toasted
$1/3$ to $1/2$ cup mayonnaise
1 teaspoon bottled smoke
1 heaping teaspoon Dijon
    mustard
Dash of Worcestershire sauce
Dash of hot pepper sauce
Black pepper
Smoked paprika

Smoked Paprika Pimiento Cheese

Before he discovered cheater BBQ, the only indoor kitchen appliance R. B. had a serious relationship with was the toaster oven. He fancies himself the master of all things topped with melted cheese. Predictably, leftovers of this smoky cheese spread went right into the toaster oven on slices of thick rustic bread. Smoky Pimiento Cheese Bruschetta!

Min took it to the next level with sliced fresh tomato, a few green onion bits, and a basil leaf for a "New South" Italian appetizer. Of course, the pimiento cheese is fantastic on a big juicy Cheater Kitchen Burger (page 119). We also serve our pimiento cheese along with Cheater Foie Gras (page 21), each spread on tart Granny Smith apple slices.

MAKES ABOUT 3 CUPS

- 8 ounces sharp white Cheddar cheese, shredded (2 cups)
- 8 ounces cream cheese, softened
- 1/4 cup mayonnaise
- 1/4 to 1/3 cup chopped roasted red peppers
- 1 teaspoon smoked paprika
- 1 teaspoon fresh lemon juice

COMBINE all the ingredients in a medium bowl using a wooden spoon or a fork. Scoop into a serving bowl or use for open-faced melted cheese sandwiches.

PIMIENTO CHEESE

There are a million ways to make this classic Southern sandwich spread. Really good pimiento (pronounced pa-MIN-ah) cheese requires a good mayonnaise, some hand-grated Cheddar, and a small jar of pimientos. Just like tuna salad (and barbecue sauce), it's re-created countless times when people add their own twist: Worcestershire and hot pepper sauces, dry or wet mustard, grated onion, a bit of sugar, sharp cheese, mild cheese, Velveeta, cream cheese, and chopped pimiento-stuffed olives.

In this recipe, Min likes how the cream cheese disperses the smoked paprika throughout the spread. Roasted red peppers, a trendy new ingredient in pimiento cheese, also contribute to the earthy flavor.

Cheater Foie Gras

Recipes, like everything else fashionable, rise and fall with popular perception. They're in, they're out, they're hot, they're hopelessly last season.

Liver has never caught the wave of coolness, unless it's taken from a force-fed goose. Even liver as haute couture as foie gras is on the OUT list, branded as inhumane and even outlawed in some places.

Slumming with ready-to-wear liverwurst, on the other hand, is looking pretty fresh. Why shouldn't it? Liverwurst has plenty in common with foie gras, especially its color and buttery smoothness when it's blended with cream cheese. Instead of slapping it on rye bread with mustard, serve it with the sweet flavors that commonly adorn foie gras, and your perception will instantly change. This is absolutely one of R. B.'s favorite cheater recipes.

MAKES 2 CUPS

8 ounces braunschweiger, softened

8 ounces cream cheese, softened

1 tablespoon coarse-grained mustard

1 tablespoon bottled smoke

Dash of hot pepper sauce

For serving

Melba toast or crackers of your choice

Green apple slices, dates, or figs

Hot pepper jelly, fig or cherry preserves, orange marmalade, and/or smoked paprika for garnish

COMBINE the braunschweiger, cream cheese, mustard, bottled smoke, and hot pepper sauce in a medium bowl and blend together with a fork until creamy.

PILE the mixture in a crock or bowl. Cover and chill until serving time.

SERVE as a spread with toasts, fruit, and your choice of garnishes.

Hot Peño Noir Spinach Cheese Dip

Hummus may come and go, but warm spinach cheese dip, with its highly satiating qualities and homey familiarity, is still and always will be an excellent choice for casual parties involving cocktails. Broiler-charred jalapeños are our spin to bump this old classic into flavor advanced placement. As with any creamy cheese spread, R. B. will find any leftovers, no matter how buried in Min's fridge, to plop on open-faced burgers.

MAKES 8 SERVINGS

4 fresh jalapeño peppers

Vegetable oil

One 10-ounce box frozen chopped spinach, thawed and squeezed dry

8 ounces smoked Cheddar cheese, shredded (2 cups)

8 ounces cream cheese, softened

1/4 cup mayonnaise

1 tablespoon Worcestershire sauce

1 tablespoon fresh lemon juice

Kosher salt

Crackers and/or tortilla chips

HEAT the broiler.

CUT the jalapeños in half lengthwise. Place them in a small roasting pan and drizzle lightly with oil.

BROIL the peppers about 4 inches from the heat source until soft and slightly charred, turning occasionally, 8 to 10 minutes. Remove from the oven and lower the heat to 400°F.

When the peppers are cool, REMOVE the stems and seeds with the tip of a knife. Finely chop the peppers.

COMBINE the peppers, spinach, cheeses, mayonnaise, Worcestershire sauce, and lemon juice in a large bowl and blend well. Add salt to taste.

SPREAD the mixture in a pie plate. Bake for 20 to 30 minutes, until heated through and lightly browned and bubbly. Serve with crackers and tortilla chips.

Any Smoked Fish Party Spread

These days quality hardwood-smoked salmon and trout in convenient Cryovac packages are easy to find. What we never expected was that even canned tuna, a product that has required little contemplation beyond water- versus oil-packed,

would go through a major transformation with the new retort vacuum-packed foil pouch. No can opener, no draining, and new flavors to play with. A pouch or two of hickory-smoked tuna works for this spread.

When we say any fish, we mean any fish or any shellfish, like smoked oysters or clams. We usually use a frozen pack of R. B.'s patio-smoked, fresh-caught Rhode Island bluefish courtesy of his friend and neighbor Chappy Pierce. Vary the ratio of seafood to cream cheese to your liking. If things taste fishy, add lemon juice. Serve the spread mounded in a bowl garnished with capers and lemon slices. We prefer plain water crackers for serving.

MAKES 3 CUPS

8 to 12 ounces smoked fish or shellfish

8 ounces cream cheese, softened

1/4 cup finely chopped red onion

1/4 cup finely chopped celery

1/4 cup chopped fresh parsley

1 to 2 tablespoons fresh lemon juice

2 teaspoons Dijon mustard

1 to 2 tablespoons capers

Water crackers

PLACE the fish in a medium bowl. Break it up with a fork, if necessary.

ADD the cream cheese and blend the mixture together. Stir in the onion, celery, parsley, lemon juice, and mustard.

COVER and refrigerate until serving. Garnish with capers and serve with water crackers.

Cheesy Alligator Snouts

In spite of his Irish tendencies to worry and brood, R. B. pretends to think of himself as an upbeat guy who genuinely wants to like things. Even so, he's given up on grilled shrimp-stuffed jalapeño peppers. It's hard to cook a raw shrimp tucked inside a pepper unless the pepper is roasted to bitter death.

MAKES 12 PEPPERS

12 fresh jalapeño peppers and/or mini red and yellow sweet bell peppers

¼ pound Monterey or pepper Jack cheese

Tortilla chips (optional)

Cheesy alligator snouts—broiled and blistered jalapeños with melted cheese—never disappoint. Broil or toaster-oven these treats and all they need as garnish is plenty of cold beer.

Serve the broiled snouts as a conversation-starting appetizer, whole and hot from the oven, or sliced and set in little tortilla scoops. Serve them as a side to a Mexican feast paired with Cheater Carne Adovada Alinstante (page 56).

Jalapeños are usually tolerably hot, although it's impossible to know until you take a bite. Satisfy all your guests with a combination of hot green jalapeños and the mild mini red and yellow sweet bell peppers.

HEAT the broiler. Slice each jalapeño lengthwise, leaving the stem on. If you like, remove the seeds and membranes with the handle of a teaspoon.

SLICE the cheese to fit inside the peppers. Divide the cheese among the peppers and secure the pepper halves together with a toothpick.

BROIL about 4 inches from the heat source to melt the cheese and lightly blister the pepper skin, about 10 minutes. Turn them occasionally with tongs.

SERVE the snouts whole or slice them and serve on tortilla chips.

Roasted Eggplant White Bean Spread

Have we cheesed you out? Take a cheese break and try this straight vegetable-bean puree with nutty sweet garlic and smoked paprika. It may not be the lead-off dish to a night of Crock Dogs, but it fashionably introduces dressier barbecue dinners. We especially like it with Tandoori BBQ Chicken Thighs (page 96), Cider-Soy Pork Tenderloin (page 79), House Lamb Shanks (page 128), and Ultimate Cheater Oven-Smoked Salmon (page 132).

HEAT the oven to 450°F.

SLICE off the stem of the garlic, revealing the tops of the cloves. Place the garlic and whole eggplant in a covered casserole (ceramic or enamel-coated cast iron).

COVER and roast until the eggplant is very soft when pierced with a fork and the garlic looks golden brown, about 30 minutes.

REMOVE the casserole from the oven, uncover, and cool the vegetables enough to handle.

CUT open the eggplant, scrape out the flesh, and place it in a food processor. Discard the eggplant skin.

SQUEEZE the roasted cloves from the garlic skins and place them in the bowl with the eggplant. Add the beans, lemon juice, paprika, and salt to taste and process until smooth.

CUT the pita bread into triangles. Lay them on a baking sheet and toast in a hot (450°F) oven until lightly browned.

DRIZZLE the spread with olive oil, sprinkle with parsley and additional paprika, and serve with the pita.

....

MAKES ABOUT 3 CUPS

2 whole garlic heads

1 medium eggplant

One 19-ounce can cannellini beans, drained and rinsed (you can use any white beans)

2 to 3 tablespoons fresh lemon juice (or the juice of 1 lemon)

2 teaspoons smoked paprika, plus more for garnish

Kosher salt

Pita bread

Olive oil

Chopped fresh parsley

CHEATER BEGINNINGS

Hot-Oven Garlic Heads

In addition to seasoning the Roasted Eggplant White Bean Spread (page 25), roasted garlic with a little smoke adds great flavor to hummus, mashed potatoes, and butter or olive oil spread on bread or over a steak. Blend roasted garlic with some mayonnaise for burgers and sandwiches.

2 whole garlic heads
Olive oil
Bottled smoke
Kosher salt

HEAT the oven to 450°F.

SLICE off the stem of the garlic, revealing the tops of the cloves. Place the garlic on a sheet of aluminum foil large enough to seal around the heads. Drizzle with oil and sprinkle lightly with bottled smoke.

SEAL the packet and bake for 45 minutes to 1 hour. The garlic is cooked when golden brown and very tender.

When the heads are cool enough to handle, SQUEEZE the soft garlic paste out of the papery skin into a small bowl. Season with salt to taste.

Hot-Oven Drums

Like fried chicken and good corn bread, oven drums are all about the crust. The key to Hot-Oven Drums is to get the skin working for you. Hot-Oven Drums are inspired by Nashville's cultish hot pan-fried chicken that's dusted-to-dredged in cayenne pepper. Proceed with caution!

Here the skillet meets the oven. The bread crumbs, dry rub, and oil keep the Hot-Oven Drums crisp and the cayenne pepper, added right before cooking, lets you control the heat. Serve the drums just like chicken wings with ranch or blue cheese dressing and celery and carrot sticks. Eat them on your feet with a beer in the other hand and no worries about the red mess all over your face and hands.

MAKES ABOUT 15 DRUMS

3 tablespoons Cheater Basic Dry Rub (page 45)

¼ cup fine dry bread crumbs

4 pounds chicken wings or drumsticks, rinsed and patted dry

¼ cup vegetable oil

Cayenne pepper

HEAT the oven to 400°F.

COMBINE the dry rub and the bread crumbs in a wide shallow bowl.

PLACE the chicken on a large rimmed baking sheet. Drizzle the oil over the chicken and turn the pieces to coat evenly. Dredge each piece in the seasoned crumbs, coating evenly.

RETURN the chicken to the baking sheet and sprinkle with cayenne to taste.

BAKE uncovered for 30 minutes, until the internal temperature reaches at least 180°F.

Rooster Riblets

An Arctic cold snap certainly inspires one to rethink the traditional all-day hickory-smoked approach to barbecued ribs, especially with a 10°F wind chill outside and football and a roaring fire inside.

1/4 cup Cheater Basic Dry Rub (page 45)

2 tablespoons brown sugar

2 racks baby back pork ribs (2 to 3 pounds each), membrane removed (see page 64)

For the sauce

1/2 cup hoisin sauce

1/2 cup ketchup

1/4 cup dry sherry

1/4 cup rice wine vinegar

1 tablespoon dry mustard

1 tablespoon toasted sesame oil

1 large garlic clove, chopped

1 tablespoon grated fresh ginger

Saucy Asian-style Rooster Riblets were named when we first made them for Chinese New Year, then the Year of the Rooster. Rename them annually, throw them in the oven, set the timer, and relocate your cooking post to the recliner. Even better, cook them a couple days in advance. Before serving, reheat the ribs with their sauce for a few minutes in the oven, on a grill, or under the broiler to add a little crust.

Chinese ribs aren't a good match for the usual baked beans, potato salad, and creamy slaw. If you're up for it, serve pan-fried dumplings (find them in the grocery freezer section) or rice and an icy rice vinegar–cucumber salad (page 153).

HEAT the oven to 300°F.

COMBINE the dry rub and brown sugar in a small bowl.

PLACE the ribs on a large sheet of heavy-duty aluminum foil set on a large baking sheet. Coat both sides of the racks generously with the dry rub mixture. Seal the foil over the ribs.

ROAST the ribs for 1 1/2 hours. Open the foil and check for doneness. If you prefer more fall-off-the-bone tenderness, rewrap and roast for another 15 to 30 minutes.

While the ribs roast, COMBINE all the sauce ingredients in a small saucepan. Simmer for a few minutes. Warm the sauce before using.

REMOVE the ribs from the oven and cut into individual riblets. Heat the broiler. Brush the ribs with the sauce.

BROIL the ribs about 4 inches from the heat source until the sauce caramelizes, about 5 minutes. Watch carefully, because the sauce will begin to char. Or, finish them on a medium hot grill for 8 to 10 minutes, turning the ribs often with tongs. Brush the ribs with more warm sauce and continue to grill until the sauce caramelizes, about 5 minutes. (The ribs may be made ahead up to this point.)

If rewarming the ribs, WRAP them in foil and place in a 350°F oven until heated through, about 15 minutes.

Quick Sticks

A heavy little cast-iron hibachi is R. B.'s favorite outdoor grill for fast and efficient high-heat cooking. Indoors, that efficiency is called the broiler. Both tools use direct high heat to sear tender cuts of meat hot and fast. It's just that the broiler heats from above, the grill from below. Even better, the broiler gets burning hot in minutes with the turn of a knob.

Quick Sticks are a very loose version of Thai satay—thin cuts of chicken and steak rubbed with curry, threaded onto skewers, and quickly broiled. The dipping sauce is first-class cheating—barbecue sauce with some chopped peanuts thrown in. Icy Q-Cumbers (page 153) are a Quick Sticks must.

MAKES 10 TO 12 SKEWERS

2 tablespoons Cheater Indian Rub (page 46)

2 teaspoons sugar

1½ pounds boneless, skinless chicken breast halves (about 3) or thighs (about 6)

1½ pounds beef sirloin or rib eye steak, ½ inch thick

1 cup barbecue sauce

½ cup finely chopped peanuts

If using wooden skewers, **SOAK** them for at least 30 minutes before assembling the sticks. Heat the broiler.

BLEND the dry rub and sugar in a small bowl and set aside.

Using a mallet or heavy saucepan, **POUND** the chicken between two pieces of plastic wrap until it is an even ½ inch thick.

CUT the chicken and steak into strips 1 to 1½ inches wide. Thread the meat lengthwise onto the skewers. Sprinkle with the dry rub mix.

BROIL the meat 4 inches from the heat source until the chicken is cooked through, about 5 minutes per side. For rare beef, shorten the total broiling time to 7 to 8 minutes.

COMBINE the barbecue sauce and peanuts and serve at the table as a dipping sauce.

Broiled Kielbasa and Pineapple Picks

*D*ating back at least to the 1950s is a party classic known as sweet-and-sour *meatballs, or smoky sausages in an easy blend of mustard and jelly. We've seen signature variations on this theme using just about every flavor of jelly and mustard around. In the end, they all work the same, producing an easy sweet-and-sour sauce for the meat to bathe in.*

R. B.'s Aunt Kate, a veteran hostess and merrymaking ringleader in Melbourne, Florida, gives particularly high marks to dishes like this that score lowest in effort and highest in empty bowl at cocktail-recipe swap meets. Our somewhat Asian fusion variation calls for broiled fresh pineapple and kielbasa.

MAKES 12 TO 14 SERVINGS

1 pound smoked kielbasa, cut into $1/4$-inch slices

1 medium fresh pineapple, peeled, cored, and cut into chunks

One 8-ounce can whole water chestnuts, cut in half

For the sauce

$1/2$ cup apple jelly

$1/4$ cup spicy brown mustard

1 tablespoon soy sauce

HEAT the broiler.

PLACE the kielbasa slices on a large rimmed baking sheet. Broil for 10 minutes, stirring occasionally, until slightly charred.

ADD the pineapple chunks and water chestnuts and broil for an additional 5 minutes, until the fruit is slightly charred.

To make the sauce, **COMBINE** the jelly, mustard, and soy sauce in a small saucepan over medium heat. Stir until the jelly is melted and the sauce is smooth and well blended.

TRANSFER the kielbasa, pineapple, and water chestnuts to a serving bowl. Drizzle with the warm sauce and serve with toothpicks.

Cheater BBQ Pitchers

When it's party time in Cheaterland, we mix our drinks like we mix our dry rubs—supersize. You'll need several large drink pitchers for these full-size cocktails and punches. For a crowd, pick one special drink and make it ahead. When anyone asks for variety, tell them to help themselves to a cold can out of the cooler. A great party starts with a well-prepared host.

. . . .

Cheata Rita Pitcher

Cheaper spring break brands of tequila are plenty good enough for mixing with tangy sour juices and margarita mix. To prove this point to ourselves and save some money, we set up a blind Cheata Rita taste test, comparing regular cheap tequila with fancy top-shelf $45-a-bottle brands. Honestly, we could not taste a difference. You're probably thinking that we've oversmoked our taste buds, and you may be right. If so, that's money in the bank, as we're now saving the good stuff to pour over ice.

We say go economy on the tequila and perk up the margarita mix with fresh lime and orange juices.

MAKES 12 SERVINGS
One 750-ml bottle tequila
One 750-ml bottle margarita mix
1 cup fresh lime juice (reserve the wedges)
1 cup fresh orange juice
Kosher salt

COMBINE the tequila, margarita mix, and juices in a gallon-size pitcher.

MOISTEN the rims of glasses with the lime wedges you squeezed for juice. Sprinkle some kosher salt on a saucer. Spin the glass rims in the salt. Fill the glasses with ice and pour the Rita mixture over the ice.

Sparkling Sangria

Cava is cheap but good Spanish sparkling wine. It makes a festive version of sangria.

MAKES 6 TO 8 SERVINGS

1 bottle cheap sparkling wine, such as Spanish Cava or California sparkling wine
$\frac{1}{2}$ cup triple sec
1 orange, cut into thin slices
1 lime, cut into thin slices
Mint leaves

COMBINE all the ingredients in a large pitcher. Serve over ice in tall glasses.

Hazy Mary

While at first blush it may appear that this cheater pitcher was inspired by Jimi Hendrix and Creedence Clearwater Revival, the credit belongs entirely to bottled smoke. Rim the glasses with Cheater Basic Smoked Salt with celery seed (page 48) if you like.

MAKES 16 SERVINGS

One 750-ml bottle vodka or tequila or four 12-ounce beers
Two 1-quart bottles Clamato juice
$\frac{1}{4}$ cup Worcestershire sauce
3 tablespoons bottled smoke
Juice of 4 lemons or limes
3 tablespoons Old Bay seasoning
Hot pepper sauce, to taste
Celery sticks

COMBINE all the ingredients (except the celery) in a gallon jug. Serve over ice in tall glasses, garnished with celery sticks.

Sparkling Shandy

Lemonade and champagne are among our top choices to serve with barbecue, so we mixed them together for an unusual shandy.

MAKES 8 SERVINGS

1 bottle cheap sparkling wine, such as Spanish Cava or California sparkling wine
2 cups lemonade
1 lemon, cut into thin slices

COMBINE all the ingredients in a large pitcher. Serve in champagne flutes.

....

Red Zingria

As a grilled-food guy, R. B. loves red Zinfandel and Côtes du Rhone. Mixed with fresh fruit and carbonation, these barbecue-friendly reds really come to life. Sweeten with sugar if you like.

MAKES 8 SERVINGS

1 bottle red Zinfandel
$\frac{1}{2}$ cup triple sec
1 lemon, cut into thin slices
1 orange, cut into thin slices
About 2 cups soda water

COMBINE all the ingredients in a large pitcher. Serve over ice in tall glasses.

....

Cheater Hot Cider

Back in the day when Min and her pal Philip Bernard attended Virginia Tech football pregame tailgate parties with fervent religiosity, a touch of special cider was often the incentive for warming up some team spirit. In truth, there is absolutely nothing Hokie about this fine cider punch, what with the assistance of the special team's Tennessee whiskey and all.

MAKES 16 SERVINGS

2 quarts apple cider

1 cup fresh orange juice

4 cinnamon sticks

8 whole cloves

8 whole allspice

One 750-ml bottle Tennessee whiskey

1 cup triple sec

POUR the apple cider and orange juice into a large slow cooker (at least 5 quarts).

TIE the cinnamon, cloves, and allspice in a piece of cheesecloth and drop the bundle in the slow cooker. Cover and heat on low until warm.

Just before serving, ADD the whiskey and the triple sec. Keep the slow cooker on the warm or low setting during the party. Serve in mugs.

. . . .

Eye-Patch Punch

Even the most modest imbibers insist on a taste of this spiced rum punch. It does indeed pack a punch, so serve with caution.

MAKES ABOUT 50 SERVINGS

One 1³/4-liter bottle spiced rum

Four 64-ounce cartons orange-pineapple juice

One 8-ounce bottle Rose's lime juice

COMBINE all the ingredients in a large orange Home Depot cooler or other colorful drink dispenser/cooler. Serve over ice in tall glasses.

CHAPTER 2

Cheater BBQ Sauces, Rubs, and Home-Smoked Salt Blends

East I-40 Vinegar Cheater Q Sauce

I-40 Pink Vinegar Cheater Q Sauce

I-25 Smoky Cheater Q Sauce

I-20 Mustardy Cheater Q Sauce

Nashville Crossroads Cheater Q Sauce

I-70 Cheater Q Sauce

I-35 Chili Cheater Q Sauce

I-5 Asian Cheater Q Sauce

Cheater Basic Dry Rub

Cheater Chili Dry Rub

Cheater Rib and Pork Rub

Cheater Indian Rub

Cheater Chinese Dry Rub

Cheater Jamaican Jerk Rub

Cheater Rub de la Maison

Cheater Smoked Rub

Cheater No-Salt Dry Rub

Cheater Basic Smoked Salt

Smoked Paprika Salt

Cheater Smoked Sweet Salt

Interstate Cheater Q Sauces

Our cheater barbecue sauce collection takes you from North Carolina to California, representing the regional styles as they meld and change across the country. The interstates point the way.

While we're big cheaters, we firmly believe in making our own barbecue sauces. We've pretty much tested the dizzying array of store-brand sauces and do keep some on hand. But a custom-made sauce takes only a few minutes and requires a minimum of basic ingredients.

The goal of any sauce is to balance the sweet, sour, salt, and savory tastes so that the meat will be enhanced, not hidden. There are lots of ways to do this. When you make your own, you'll see that you can have it your way. Knowing how will also help you sort out your favorite bottled sauces and even customize them. The sauces are essentially combinations of sugar, ketchup, and vinegar, so they'll stay fresh in sealed containers in the refrigerator for several weeks.

. . . .

East I-40 Vinegar Cheater Q Sauce

Eastern North Carolina's pungent vinegar sauce is accented with black pepper notes and a light sweetness, but no tomato. Because it works so well with pulled pork, its popularity has traveled way beyond the region.

MAKES ABOUT 2 CUPS

1 cup cider vinegar

3 tablespoons brown sugar

2 tablespoons Worcestershire sauce

1 teaspoon coarsely ground black pepper

1 teaspoon paprika

1 teaspoon kosher salt, or to taste

$1/2$ teaspoon cayenne pepper, or to taste

COMBINE all the ingredients in a jar with a tight-fitting lid. Shake well.

I-20 Mustardy Cheater Q Sauce

Farther south in South Carolina and Georgia, tangy yellow mustard predominates.

MAKES ABOUT 2 CUPS

1 small onion, grated

2 tablespoons vegetable oil

1 cup prepared yellow mustard

1/4 cup ketchup

1/2 cup brown sugar

1/2 cup cider vinegar

1 teaspoon coarsely ground black pepper

1/2 teaspoon cayenne pepper, or to taste

1 teaspoon kosher salt, or to taste

COOK the onion in the oil in a small saucepan over medium heat until tender, about 5 minutes. Stir in the remaining ingredients. Simmer until thickened and smooth.

I-40 Pink Vinegar Cheater Q Sauce

Heading west toward Tennessee on I-40, Pink Vinegar is more voluptuous, kinder, and gentler thanks to a little ketchup and more sugar.

MAKES ABOUT 2 CUPS

1 cup cider vinegar

1/2 cup ketchup

1/4 cup brown sugar

2 tablespoons Worcestershire sauce

1 teaspoon coarsely ground black pepper

1 teaspoon paprika

1 teaspoon kosher salt, or to taste

1/2 teaspoon cayenne pepper, or to taste

COMBINE all the ingredients in a jar with a tight-fitting lid. Shake well.

CHEATER BBQ SAUCES, RUBS, AND HOME-SMOKED SALT BLENDS

Nashville Crossroads Cheater Q Sauce

Nashville Crossroads is an even balance of vinegar, ketchup, and sugar, combining the influences from the Carolinas to our east and from Memphis to our west. It's our number one pick to brush on Ultimate Cheater Pork Ribs (page 61) and pretty much any cheater pork. Even dry-rubbed Memphis ribs enjoy a bath at the crossroads.

MAKES ABOUT 2 CUPS

1 small onion, grated

2 tablespoons vegetable oil

1/2 cup cider vinegar

1/2 cup ketchup

1/2 cup brown sugar

2 tablespoons Worcestershire sauce

1 tablespoon bottled smoke (optional)

1 teaspoon kosher salt

1 teaspoon coarsely ground black pepper

1/2 teaspoon cayenne pepper, or to taste

COOK the onion in the oil in a small saucepan over medium heat until tender, about 5 minutes. Stir in the remaining ingredients. Simmer for a few minutes until thickened and smooth.

························

I-70 Cheater Q Sauce

Heading west toward Missouri, the sauce darkens, deepens, and sweetens, thanks to molasses and bottled smoke.

MAKES ABOUT 2 CUPS

1 small onion, grated

2 tablespoons vegetable oil

1 cup ketchup

$^{1}/_{2}$ cup molasses

$^{1}/_{4}$ cup cider vinegar

2 tablespoons Worcestershire sauce

2 to 3 tablespoons bottled smoke

1 teaspoon coarsely ground black pepper

$^{1}/_{2}$ teaspoon cayenne pepper, or to taste

1 teaspoon kosher salt, or to taste

COOK the onion in the oil in a small saucepan over medium heat until tender, about 5 minutes. Stir in the remaining ingredients. Simmer for a few minutes until thickened and smooth.

CHEATER BBQ SAUCES, RUBS, AND HOME-SMOKED SALT BLENDS

I-35 Chili Cheater Q Sauce

Moving through the Plains toward the Southwest, the sauce flattens out with more tomato, less vinegar, and a touch of chili on the horizon.

MAKES ABOUT 2 CUPS

1 small onion, grated

2 tablespoons vegetable oil

1^1/$_2$ cups ketchup

2 tablespoons brown sugar

2 tablespoons cider vinegar

2 tablespoons Worcestershire sauce

1 teaspoon coarsely ground black pepper

1 tablespoon chili powder

1 teaspoon kosher salt, or to taste

COOK the onion in the oil in a small saucepan over medium heat until tender, about 5 minutes. Stir in the remaining ingredients. Simmer for a few minutes until thickened and smooth.

I-25 Smoky Cheater Q Sauce

Heating up in the desert sun, chipotles bring the smoke; lemon takes over for the vinegar.

MAKES ABOUT 2 CUPS

1 small onion, grated

2 tablespoons vegetable oil

1^1/$_2$ cups ketchup

^{1}/$_4$ cup chopped chipotle peppers in adobo sauce

^{1}/$_4$ cup brown sugar

^{1}/$_4$ cup fresh lemon juice

1 tablespoon chili powder

1 teaspoon kosher salt, or to taste

COOK the onion in the oil in a small saucepan over medium heat until tender, about 5 minutes. Stir in the remaining ingredients. Simmer for a few minutes until thickened and smooth.

I-5 Asian Cheater Q Sauce

Three thousand miles from the Atlantic, California sauces welcome Asian influences. Honey, ginger, soy, citrus, and Asian hot pepper sauce mingle with ketchup.

MAKES ABOUT 2 CUPS

1 small onion, grated
2 tablespoons vegetable oil
3 garlic cloves, minced
2 tablespoons grated or finely chopped fresh ginger
$1/2$ cup ketchup
$1/2$ cup soy sauce
$1/2$ cup honey
$1/2$ cup fresh lemon or lime juice or red wine vinegar
2 tablespoons Asian hot pepper sauce (Rooster Sauce)

COOK the onion in the oil in a small saucepan over medium heat until tender, about 5 minutes. Stir in the remaining ingredients. Simmer for a few minutes until thickened and smooth.

CHEATER BBQ SAUCES, RUBS, AND HOME-SMOKED SALT BLENDS

DRY RUB CHEAT SHEET

Ever had bland grilled or roasted meats and wondered why? It's probably because the meat didn't get rubbed enough. Dry rubs do two things for meats, fish, and vegetables. One, they impart great flavor. Two, they add color and texture. If you have time, rub meats hours ahead for the most flavor, or sprinkle the rub at the last minute just like salt and pepper—the most elementary rub blend of all.

Making a dry rub couldn't be simpler. It's just a blend of seasonings and salt that gets literally (and liberally, at times) rubbed into the meat (or sprinkled on vegetables) before and after cooking. Don't let the gourmet store blends or your bar-b-guru's secret rub complicate things. A basic rub starts with paprika, black pepper, and kosher salt. Add whatever you like to that trio, but resist the temptation to overcomplicate a rub with too many seasonings. We keep the salt level at about one-fifth to one-quarter of the mix. Adjust the salt to suit your taste. The toughest part is probably pulling together a collection of jars.

A good rub can accent a barbecued meat or a vegetable dish brilliantly and we often skip a sauce, even with cheater ribs and chicken. Make a big batch and you're set for months. Stored properly, dry rubs keep as long as the spices in the rub stay fresh, about a year.

Rubs and Home-Smoked Salt Blends

....

Cheater Basic Dry Rub

MAKES ABOUT $2/3$ CUP

1/4 cup paprika

2 tablespoons kosher salt

2 tablespoons coarsely ground black pepper

1 tablespoon garlic powder

1 tablespoon dry mustard

COMBINE all the ingredients in a jar with a tight-fitting lid. Shake to blend.

....

Cheater Chili Dry Rub

MAKES ABOUT $2/3$ CUP

1/4 cup chili powder

2 tablespoons kosher salt

2 tablespoons coarsely ground black pepper

1 tablespoon garlic powder

1 tablespoon ground cumin

COMBINE all the ingredients in a jar with a tight-fitting lid. Shake to blend.

....

Cheater Rib and Pork Rub

ADD 1 tablespoon brown sugar to each 2 tablespoons of Cheater Basic or Cheater Chili Dry Rub.

CHEATER BBQ SAUCES, RUBS, AND HOME-SMOKED SALT BLENDS

Cheater Indian Rub

MAKES ABOUT $2/3$ CUP

$1/4$ cup curry powder, red curry powder, or garam masala

$1/4$ cup paprika

2 tablespoons kosher salt

COMBINE all the ingredients in a jar with a tight-fitting lid. Shake to blend.

Cheater Chinese Dry Rub

MAKES ABOUT $2/3$ CUP

$1/4$ cup Chinese five-spice powder

$1/4$ cup paprika

2 tablespoons kosher salt

COMBINE all the ingredients in a jar with a tight-fitting lid. Shake to blend.

Cheater Jamaican Jerk Rub

MAKES 2 CUPS

$1/2$ cup brown sugar

$1/4$ cup kosher salt

$1/4$ cup paprika

$1/4$ cup coarsely ground black pepper

2 tablespoons garlic powder

2 tablespoons dried thyme

2 tablespoons allspice

2 tablespoons dried lemon peel

COMBINE all the ingredients in a jar with a tight-fitting lid. Shake to blend.

Cheater Rub de la Maison

MAKES ABOUT 1 CUP

3 tablespoons kosher salt
$^1/_4$ cup paprika
$^1/_4$ cup coarsely ground black pepper
$^1/_4$ cup herbes de Provence
2 tablespoons dried lemon peel

COMBINE all the ingredients in a jar with a tight-fitting lid. Shake to blend.

Cheater Smoked Rub

MAKES ABOUT $^3/_4$ CUP

$^1/_4$ cup ancho chile powder
$^1/_4$ cup smoked paprika
3 tablespoons Cheater Basic Smoked Salt (page 48)
1 tablespoon garlic powder
1 tablespoon coarsely ground black pepper

COMBINE all the ingredients in a jar with a tight-fitting lid. Shake to blend.

Cheater No-Salt Dry Rub

Cheater No-Salt has dry rub flavor without the salt. It's especially useful for already brined pork, poultry, and shrimp. Of course, you can eliminate the salt in any of the cheater dry rubs and add any seasonings you like. It's your kitchen and you're in charge, so shake things up a little.

MAKES $^3/_4$ CUP

$^1/_4$ cup paprika

CHEATER BBQ SAUCES, RUBS, AND HOME-SMOKED SALT BLENDS

¹/₄ cup coarsely ground black pepper

2 tablespoons garlic powder

2 tablespoons onion powder

COMBINE all the ingredients in a jar with a tight-fitting lid. Shake to blend.

. . . .

Cheater Basic Smoked Salt

We use smoked salts on everything that begs for a nuance of mysterious flavor. The gourmet hardwood-smoked sea salts are little brown bombshells of flavor. Our simplified cheater is quick to make and lasts indefinitely. Add an herb or a spice to complement a special dish or drink, like Hazy Marys (page 33) rimmed in smoked salt with celery seed.

2 tablespoons kosher or coarse sea salt

1 teaspoon bottled smoke

COMBINE the salt and bottled smoke in a small dish or a jar. Cover. The smoked salt will keep indefinitely.

Variations
Add 1 teaspoon smoked paprika—sweet or bittersweet.

Add 1 teaspoon celery seed.

Add 1 teaspoon coarsely ground black pepper and 1 teaspoon grated lemon zest.

Add 1 teaspoon curry powder.

Add a pinch of cayenne pepper.

Smoked Paprika Salt

Extra-fine-grained popcorn salt has about the same consistency as powdery smoked paprika. The two blend beautifully together and adhere especially well to hot popcorn and French fries.

Popcorn salt (extra-fine-grained salt)
Smoked paprika

COMBINE equal amounts of popcorn salt and smoked paprika in a small jar or shaker. Keep handy to sprinkle on popcorn and vegetables.

Cheater Smoked Sweet Salt

The most sophisticated desserts combine a little salty component with the sweet. Try this crystallized yin/yang blend sprinkled on chocolate sauce, caramel, smoky s'mores, or a simple piece of chocolate for a subtle bang of unexpected flavor. A blend of coarse sugar crystals, like Demerara, with kosher salt delivers a chic look and immediate impact.

3 tablespoons coarse sugar
1 tablespoon kosher salt
1/4 teaspoon bottled smoke

COMBINE all the ingredients in a small dish.

CHEATER BBQ SAUCES, RUBS, AND HOME-SMOKED SALT BLENDS

CHAPTER 3

Cheater Pork

PULLED PORK CHEAT SHEET

For any barbecue pulled pork, cheater or not, the king cut is the Boston blade roast, or as it's better known in barbecue land, the Boston butt. Although it sounds like it comes from the rear of the hog, it's actually the upper shoulder roast. Like beef chuck roast, the Boston butt is a well-marbled, tough cut ideal for low-temperature cooking and for absorbing the flavor of smoke. As the butt cooks, the fat melts away and the meat becomes fork-tender for shredding or "pulling" into long strands, or for chopping into bits.

Look for 6- to 9-pound bone-in roasts or 4- to 7-pound boneless roasts. Generally, we've found that a pork butt will give you about half its weight in cooked and drained meat. A large 9-pound roast will fill a 5- to 7-quart slow cooker. Cut the pork butt into large chunks to fit well in the slow cooker and to shorten the cooking time.

The lower portion of the pork shoulder is the arm picnic. Even though it's a cheaper cut, it's not our favorite because there's more waste and more mess. Pulling and chopping a barbecued arm picnic involves getting rid of a large bone, a thick cap of tough skin, and plenty of fat. In the end, a 7-pound arm picnic yields only about $2\frac{1}{2}$ pounds of pulled pork. Only when a supermarket is practically giving them away do we bother with one.

Molasses Vinegar Pork Butt

Our friend Philip Bernard of Raleigh, North Carolina, has plenty of hickory-smoked barbecue options, and still he's a cheater. Philip likes to add molasses and vinegar to the pork butt to create a built-in sauce while it cooks. Be sure to trim the excess fat from raw meat in recipes like this when you want to serve the barbecue right away in its cooking liquid.

MAKES 12 TO 14 SERVINGS

3/4 cup molasses, or more if needed

1 cup cider vinegar

1/2 cup bottled smoke

One 5- to 6-pound boneless Boston butt pork roast or same weight of boneless country-style pork ribs

1/4 cup Cheater Basic Dry Rub (page 45)

POUR the molasses in the bottom of a large slow cooker (at least 5 quarts), using enough to cover the bottom. Add the vinegar and the bottled smoke.

CUT the pork butt into medium (2- to 3-inch) chunks (the ribs don't need to be cut up) and add them to the slow cooker. Sprinkle the meat with the rub, turning the pieces to coat evenly.

COVER and cook on high for 5 to 6 hours or on low for 10 to 12 hours, until the meat is pull-apart tender and reaches an internal temperature of 190°F.

Using tongs and a slotted spoon, TRANSFER the meat to a rimmed platter or baking sheet. Let rest until cool enough to handle.

PULL the meat into strands. It should shred very easily. Serve with the warm meat juices.

To serve the barbecue later, cover and REFRIGERATE the meat when it has cooled. Pour the meat juice into a separate container and refrigerate. Before reheating the juice, skim and discard the congealed fat layer on the top.

To reheat the barbecue, PLACE it in a saucepan moistened with some of the reserved juice. Gently heat the meat on medium-low, stirring occasionally. Or, place it in a covered casserole with some of the reserved juice and heat in a 350°F oven for 20 to 30 minutes.

Ultimate Cheater Pulled Pork

*O*kay, here we go. Either we have you hooked at "Ultimate Cheater Pulled Pork" or this book is headed straight for the library's used book sale. We know that. You know that. So, let's drop the chitchat and make some cheater barbecue.

MAKES 12 TO 14 SERVINGS

One 5- to 6-pound boneless Boston butt pork roast or same weight of boneless country-style pork ribs

¼ cup Cheater Basic Dry Rub (page 45)

½ cup bottled smoke

Barbeque sauce of your choice (pages 38 to 43)

In short, you drop a pork butt into the slow cooker, add dry rub and bottled smoke, close the cover, go away for a while, pull or chop the meat and pile it on a bun, add sauce, get out the pickles, open a beer. BOOM! That's barbecue, baby. Can you feel it? That's Ultimate Cheater Pulled Pork.

CUT the pork butt into medium (2- to 3-inch) chunks (the ribs don't need to be cut up).

PUT the pieces in a large slow cooker (at least 5 quarts). Sprinkle the meat with the rub, turning the pieces to coat evenly. Add the bottled smoke.

COVER and cook on high for 5 to 6 hours or on low for 10 to 12 hours, until the meat is pull-apart tender and reaches an internal temperature of 190°F.

Using tongs and a slotted spoon, TRANSFER the meat to a rimmed platter or baking sheet. Let rest until cool enough to handle.

CHEATER KNIFE-AND-FORK RIBS

Country-style pork ribs aren't ribs in the traditional sense of a long bone wrapped in meat. They're more meat than bone (if they have any bone at all), and they're best with a knife and fork, a little sauce, and some corn bread. Done in a slow cooker, these ribs melt into short-strand pulled-pork barbecue in less time than a Boston butt shoulder because the ribs come already cut. Country-style ribs give off less meat juice and less fat than the shoulder, too.

PULL the meat into strands. It should shred very easily. Serve the barbecue piled on buns with your favorite barbecue sauce.

To serve the barbecue later, cover and REFRIGERATE the meat when it has cooled. Pour the meat juice into a separate container and refrigerate. Before reheating the juice, skim and discard the congealed fat layer on the top.

To reheat the barbecue, PLACE it in a saucepan moistened with some of the reserved juice. Gently heat the meat on medium-low, stirring occasionally. Or, place it in a covered casserole with some of the reserved juice and heat in a 350°F oven for 20 to 30 minutes.

While the meat warms, COMBINE the barbecue sauce and some of the additional reserved meat juice in a saucepan. Heat through and serve with the barbecue.

. . . .

Big Oven Butt

A big pork butt cooks to pull-apart tenderness as well in an oven as in a slow cooker. It's up to you, so choose your weapon.

Heat the oven to 300°F. Place the pork butt in a large roasting pan. Coat the outsides generously with the dry rub. Pour in the bottled smoke. Cover the pan with heavy-duty aluminum foil. Roast for 5 to 8 hours, until the meat is pull-apart tender and reaches an internal temperature of 190°F.

Cheater Carne Adovada Alinstante

Our friend Mary Ellen Chavez of Belen, New Mexico, owns the wildly popular Burritos Alinstante, a small chain with a cultish following in the Albuquerque area. When he met her, R. B. (a swamp Yankee from Rhode Island) asked what kind of Mexican food she served. "We don't serve Mexican food, R. B., it's New Mexican," she gently corrected. "New Mexico is the only place for red and green chiles like ours." Serving her mother's famous burritos with New Mexico red and green chiles has earned the small chain Best of Show among more than 230 vendors at the New Mexico State Fair.

Number one on the menu is Carne Adovada, pork that's first browned or grilled, then slow-cooked in New Mexico red chile sauce. We've swapped Mary Ellen's restaurant steam pan for a slow cooker. Fortunately, dried New Mexico red chiles are available pretty much everywhere now.

To make the sauce, rehydrate the dried chiles in hot water and blend them with garlic and a little water. After a warm night in the slow cooker, you've got breakfast burritos Alinstante. Mary Ellen has yet to tire of them, but she limits herself to one a day.

MAKES 12 TO 14 SERVINGS

For the chile sauce

12 dried New Mexico chiles

5 garlic cloves

One 5- to 6-pound boneless Boston butt pork roast, cut into 1-inch pieces

2 tablespoons all-purpose flour

1 tablespoon kosher salt

To make the chile sauce, **REMOVE** the stems from the chiles. Break the chiles into pieces, place them in a medium bowl, and cover with 2 cups boiling water. Let the chiles soften, about 30 minutes.

PLACE the chiles, garlic, and about half the soaking water in a blender. Blend into a smooth paste. Add more water as necessary.

To make the pork, HEAT the oven to 450°F. Coat a large rimmed baking sheet with nonstick cooking spray.

PUT the pork cubes in a large bowl and toss them with the flour and salt. Place them on the baking sheet in one layer, without crowding. Use two baking sheets, if necessary.

ROAST the pork until it is browned and most of the fat has cooked off, about 30 minutes.

PLACE the pork in a large slow cooker (at least 5 quarts). Discard the drippings on the baking sheet. Stir in the chile sauce. Add 2 cups water to the meat mixture. Cover and cook on high for 4 to 6 hours or on low for 8 to 10 hours, until the meat is tender.

CHEATER PORK

T or C Pork

M in's uncle Mike and aunt Mary of Belen, New Mexico, spend their free time on the banks of the Rio Grande in the little resort town of Truth or Consequences. The town's name change from Hot Springs occurred back in 1950 when Ralph Edwards, host of the popular radio show, announced that, to celebrate the show's tenth anniversary, Truth or Consequences would broadcast from the first town to rename itself after the show.

....
MAKES 12 TO 14 SERVINGS

5 to 6 pounds boneless country-style pork ribs

2 medium onions, chopped

6 garlic cloves, minced

One 7-ounce can chipotle peppers in adobo sauce, chopped

$1/2$ cup cider vinegar

$1/4$ cup bottled smoke

$1/4$ cup chili powder

1 tablespoon kosher salt

2 tablespoons ground cumin

1 tablespoon dried oregano

One 6-ounce can tomato paste

Forward-thinking civic leaders jumped at the opportunity for free publicity and to instantly differentiate their town from the hundreds of other Hot Springs across the country. The name change vote passed and Ralph Edwards became a town hero. Now, everybody just calls it T or C for short.

After a day relaxing with high-speed toys on the nearby Elephant Butte Reservoir, Mike and Mary regularly welcome a brood of sunburnt kids and friends with a patio barbecue. Elaborate cooking is the last thing on anyone's mind. This throw-it-all-in-the-slow-cooker chili pork barbecue (or try it with beef chuck roast) lets Mary have as much fun as the rest of the gang. Serve the meat with warm tortillas, guacamole, shredded lettuce, onions, and plenty of Pecos Pintos (page 147).

COMBINE all the ingredients in a large slow cooker (at least 6 quarts) and stir until well blended.

COVER and cook on high for 5 to 6 hours or on low for 10 to 12 hours, until the meat is pull-apart tender and reaches an internal temperature of 190°F.

USE tongs to serve the meat right out of the slow cooker.

Luau Pork

*I*n between cruises when you're pining for the late-night lido deck scene, there's no better way to escape the quotidian than an island-themed luau.

Lining the slow cooker with banana leaves and filling it with seasoned pork can really generate a breezy mood. The cheater way is to put a whole banana, skin and all, on top of our Luau Pork during cooking. It gets the party point across just as well. To carry the theme, think side dishes with tropical fruits, macadamia nuts, coconut, and rice.

···

MAKES 12 TO 14 SERVINGS

One 5- to 6-pound boneless
  Boston butt pork roast or
  same weight of boneless
  country-style pork ribs

1/4 cup Cheater Basic Dry Rub
  (page 45)

1 cup pineapple juice

1 cup soy sauce

1 cup rice vinegar

1/2 cup bottled smoke

6 garlic cloves, minced

3 serrano chiles, chopped

1/4 cup shredded or chopped
  fresh ginger

1 banana, unpeeled

CUT the pork butt into medium (2- to 3-inch) chunks (the ribs don't need to be cut up).

PUT the pork in a large slow cooker (at least 6 quarts). Sprinkle the meat with the rub, turning the pieces to coat evenly. Add the pineapple juice, soy sauce, vinegar, bottled smoke, garlic, chiles, and ginger. Place the whole banana on top of the meat.

COVER and cook on high for 5 to 6 hours or on low for 8 to 10 hours, until the meat is pull-apart tender and reaches an internal temperature of 190°F.

DISCARD the banana. Using tongs and a slotted spoon, transfer the meat to a rimmed platter or baking sheet. Let rest until cool enough to handle. Pull the meat into strands. It should shred very easily.

To serve the barbecue later, COVER and refrigerate the meat when it has cooled. Pour the meat juice into a separate container and refrigerate. Before reheating the juice, skim and discard the congealed fat layer on the top.

To reheat the barbecue, PLACE it in a saucepan moistened with some of the reserved juice. Gently heat the meat on medium-low, stirring occasionally. Or, place it in a covered casserole with some of the reserved juice and heat in a 350°F oven for 20 to 30 minutes.

College Boy Helper

Even a cook-while-you-sleep cheater pork butt may require too much time, skill, and kitchen equipment for some. Here's instant gratification for those taking the scenic route to adulthood, busily mastering skill sets beyond the kitchen. College Boy Helper takes the most direct route to a hot, satisfying barbecued pork sandwich. Dude, it's awesome.

....

MAKES 2 TO 3 SERVINGS

1 pound ground pork or ground beef

1 tablespoon Cheater Basic Dry Rub (page 45)

1 tablespoon bottled smoke

¼ to ½ cup barbecue sauce

White bread or buns

Dill pickle chips

COMBINE the pork and the dry rub in a large skillet. Cook over medium-high heat until cooked through and lightly browned.

STIR in the bottled smoke and the barbecue sauce and cook until hot and bubbly.

SERVE piled on white bread with dill pickles.

Ultimate Cheater Pork Ribs

We don't understand why pork ribs are too often confined to summer barbecues, outdoor festivals, and dinner at a rib joint. At $15 to $20 a restaurant rack, maybe it's the cost. But at half the per-pound price of rib eyes, filets, and strip steaks, cost can't be the whole story.

We think ribs are just another casualty of barbecue hype and mystique, a victim of their own popularity. The result is that lots of folks are reluctant to make them at home. Can they be any good if they're not from a "real pit barbecue" restaurant, a competition team with matching shirts and dancing pig logo, or the crazy guy down the street with six grills and a smoker on wheels? Truth is, we should all be making ribs and having them with champagne, another enjoyment unfortunately confined to special occasions.

If you're a reluctant ribber, or still recovering from disappointing attempts, the cheater oven method will lead you to really great "fall-off-the-bone" spare- and baby back ribs with consistent results and minimal hassle. No lie.

....

MAKES 6 TO 8 SERVINGS

1/4 cup Cheater Basic Dry Rub (page 45)

2 tablespoons brown sugar

3 racks baby back pork ribs (6 pounds), membrane removed (see page 64)

1/4 cup bottled smoke

Barbecue sauce of your choice (pages 38 to 43)

HEAT the oven to 325°F.

MIX the dry rub with the brown sugar in a small bowl.

PLACE each baby back rack on a large (24 to 30 inches long) sheet of heavy-duty aluminum foil. Brush each rack with a light coating of bottled smoke. Spread the sweet rub over both sides of each rack. Seal the racks in the foil. (If time allows, refrigerate them for a few hours or overnight.)

PLACE the sealed racks on a couple of baking sheets and put them in the oven. While the ribs are cooking, make some barbecue sauce and set it aside.   *(continued)*

After 1$\frac{1}{2}$ hours, **PULL** out the ribs and carefully unseal the foil. The escaping steam will be hot. Cut into a rib or two and check the meat for doneness and tenderness. If you prefer more tender meat that pulls away from the bone with less resistance, reseal the foil and put the ribs back in the oven for 15 to 30 minutes.

When the ribs are done to your liking, **TAKE** them out of the oven to serve or to sauce. If saucing, turn on the oven broiler. Unseal the foil, pour off the meat juice, and discard it. Brush some of the sauce onto the ribs. Broil the ribs about 4 inches from the heat source for about 5 minutes. Watch carefully while the sauce caramelizes and do not allow it to burn.

LAY the ribs on a cutting board and separate them into sections of 1 to 4 ribs. Serve with the remaining sauce on the side.

RACCOON RIBS

For a winter barbecue a few years ago, we sprang for thirty racks of baby backs. R. B. started smoking on Wednesday so that by Saturday, the day of the party, we would be free to prep the house and lay out the food and drinks, without being exhausted. By Friday night the garage fridge was full, so the last dozen racks went into a big cooler by the back door with a heavy Dutch oven holding down the lid. Things were going according to plan.

In the morning, Min noticed some red-stained foil on the patio. We took our coffee outside to investigate, and our jaws hit the concrete. Except for a Dutch oven, the cooler was empty.

A clever little bandit had raised the weighted lid just high enough for the Dutch oven to slide into the cooler, shooting the lid across the patio. No ribs, no foil, not even a bone.

Attempting to calm R. B., Min gently suggested that we buy ribs to go and finish them with our own sauce. With his ego on the line, R. B. said no way to serving someone else's ribs.

With ten hours to party time he started over, leaving everything else for Min to do. We didn't think we had any other choice. The ribs got cooked, the party was great, and we were exhausted.

Today, we cannot believe that at no point did either of us consider cooking the ribs in the oven with some rub and bottled smoke and finishing them on the grill at the party. It never crossed our minds.

Since then, whenever we're feeding a big crowd, it's either three days outside with the smokers or an afternoon inside with the oven. The oven usually wins. For the party patio show, R. B. puts on an apron, pours on the sauce, and chars the ribs in a blaze of glory. Everyone gathers around the cutting board, beer in one hand and rib in the other. Even we get to have fun.

CHEATER PORK

PORK RIB CHEAT SHEET

All pork ribs come from the loin or the side/belly of the pig. They differ in the length of the bone and the amount of meat between the bones. Pork loin ribs (baby back ribs) have short bones and the most meat, and usually include 12 to 14 bones in a $2^1/2$- to 3-pound rack. Spareribs are cut from the lower side of the rib section near the belly. They have longer bones and a little less meat than loin ribs, and a little more fat as well. Spareribs with the brisket bone removed and the ends squared off are called St. Louis–style ribs. Spareribs have about 12 bones to a 3- to 4-pound rack.

REMOVING THE MEMBRANE
FROM A RACK OF RIBS

The thin membrane from the underside (the bone side) of a rack of ribs is tough and chewy and is worth pulling off before cooking. It's easier than it sounds and, with a little practice, takes but a minute. First, get a finger, the tip of a knife, or the handle of a spoon between the membrane and the meat right at the edge of a bone and lift up. The membrane is slippery and will resist being separated from the rack. Using a paper towel to get a good grip on it, hold the rack firmly on the counter and pull the membrane off. If it tears, grab another corner and keep pulling until all or most of it comes off.

UNDER- AND OVERCOOKED RIBS

If after an hour and a half or so the ribs are still tough and resist being pulled apart, they need more cooking time. As long as the ribs are covered or wrapped in foil and the temperature is low, the ribs will become tender with more time. Ribs can dry out like a lean pork chop if they're treated like a pork chop—too much heat and no cover.

Ribs can also be cooked or reheated for too long, beyond the much-acclaimed "fall off the bone" state to the "fall completely apart" state. There's not much sense in paying for the bone if you're not going to use it. While there is no golden rule here, our general advice is to keep the heat low, 325°F or less, and check the ribs periodically. Much past two hours and the meat on most ribs, whether spare, loin, or country style, starts to leave the bone and shred. A few practice runs and you'll dial in the times for your oven and preference.

COOK AHEAD, REHEAT, SAUCE, AND FINISH

We are big fans of cooking barbecue a day or two ahead. R. B. thinks barbecue tastes better (especially to the cook) after some time in the refrigerator. Chilling is helpful for clean cutting and removing excess fat. It also allows the cook to step away from the dish and really enjoy it later.

For ribs, we cut the chilled racks into 3- to 4-bone sections before reheating and saucing. Reheat foil-wrapped ribs in a 325°F oven for about 30 minutes. Even if you like your ribs dry, all ribs are best with a little finishing under a broiler or on a grill for a chewy outer crust. Rather than using a brush to apply the sauce, R. B.'s trick is to dunk the cut rib sections in a pot of warm sauce for instant coverage. Then the ribs are grilled or broiled 4 inches from the heat source just until the sauce bubbles and starts to char. The timing depends on the heat of your grill or broiler. Above all, watch carefully, turn them with tongs, and do not walk away. The sauce can quickly burn and become bitter.

Chinese Restaurant BBQ Ribs

Chinese ribs were oven ribs long before oven ribs were cool, as of course we all agree they now are. They've never had to suffer the embarrassment of being dragged off the patio and into the kitchen. Their only taste of the outdoors is with the delivery guy.

Cooked right in the sauce, uncovered on a baking sheet instead of wrapped in foil, the rib meat has a nice chewy bite. Chinese chili sauce brings home the flavor. You can find some in the international section of a well-stocked supermarket. The bright red-orange sauce is thick and sweet like ketchup, and hot like pepper sauce (but not as vinegary). Substitute ketchup if you like less heat. Double or triple the recipe whenever possible.

MAKES 2 TO 3 SERVINGS

1 rack baby back pork ribs
   (2 to 3 pounds), membrane
   removed (see page 64)

2 teaspoons kosher salt

1/2 cup honey

1/4 cup hot Chinese chili sauce
   (sriracha) or ketchup

1/4 cup soy sauce

2 tablespoons rice vinegar

2 garlic cloves, minced

1 tablespoon chopped fresh
   ginger

1 to 2 tablespoons sesame
   seeds, toasted (see Note)

HEAT the oven to 350°F.

CUT the ribs into 1- to 3-rib sections. Place the ribs in a roasting pan or on a large rimmed baking sheet and sprinkle with salt.

To make the sauce, COMBINE the honey, chili sauce, soy sauce, vinegar, garlic, and ginger in a small bowl. Pour the sauce over the ribs and toss until well coated.

BAKE the ribs uncovered for 1 hour, basting periodically with the accumulated drippings. Check for doneness. The rib meat should be chewy-tender and start to pull away from the bone.

SPRINKLE the ribs with the sesame seeds.

Note: To toast sesame seeds, sprinkle them in a small skillet. Cook over medium heat, stirring frequently, until lightly browned, 3 to 5 minutes. We cheat and buy them already toasted at well-stocked supermarkets and specialty grocery stores.

Hot Pot Country-Style Ribs

Y ou can't pick them up with your fingers or gnaw the bones, but country-style boneless "ribs" make nice pork barbecue. We like this hot-covered-pot-in-the-oven method to speed things up without sacrificing taste or tenderness. Moisture and smoke are trapped inside and the pork's fat keeps the meat from drying out. If you're among the 20 percent of households without a slow cooker, this is for you.

2 to 3 tablespoons cheater dry rub (you pick, pages 45 to 47)

3 pounds boneless country-style pork ribs

2 to 3 tablespoons bottled smoke

HEAT the oven to 500°F.

PLACE a large enamel-coated cast-iron pot or Dutch oven (about 7 quarts) with its lid in the oven for 15 to 20 minutes. The pot should be piping hot. Meanwhile, work the dry rub into all sides of the ribs.

Carefully PLACE the ribs in the hot pot, add the bottled smoke, cover, and immediately reduce the oven temperature to 300°F. Cook the ribs for 1 hour, or until the meat is tender and the internal temperature is 190°F.

Cheater Spares

Spareribs in the slow cooker? We first tried this method simply to rule it out for Cheater BBQ. We figured the ribs would come out gray and soggy, more like a slow cooker stew. We couldn't have been happier in our disappointment when the ribs turned out better than okay. In fact, they were handsomely browned and crusted with tender, not soggy, meat. A big 6- to 7-quart slow cooker will do two good-size racks of spare or St. Louis ribs, and you can be multitasking elsewhere. (If you actually like using the oven, you can finish them with a sauce in the oven or under the broiler.)

MAKES 6 TO 8 SERVINGS

2 racks spare or St. Louis–style pork ribs (about 8 pounds), membrane removed (see page 64)

1/4 cup Cheater Basic Dry Rub (page 45) blended with 2 tablespoons brown sugar

1/2 cup bottled smoke

Barbecue sauce (optional; you pick, pages 38 to 43)

CUT the ribs into 2- to 3-bone sections with a sharp knife.

RUB the ribs with the dry rub blend and pile them in a large slow cooker (at least 6 quarts).

POUR the bottled smoke over the ribs. Cover and cook on high for 5 to 6 hours or on low for 8 to 10 hours. Serve as is or finish with a sauce.

To finish with a sauce, BRUSH the ribs with barbecue sauce.

BAKE in a 450°F oven for about 10 minutes or place them under the broiler about 4 inches from the heat source until the sauce has caramelized and cooks onto the ribs, 5 to 7 minutes.

Mediterranean Baby Backs

I f you love ribs, it's hard to break the habit of the classic barbecue profile of brown sugar, vinegar, and ketchup. Since we can't easily find lamb ribs in Nashville, we cheat by dressing up pork ribs with Mediterranean herbs, garlic, and mustard.

1 rack baby back pork or lamb ribs (2 to 3 pounds), membrane removed (see page 64)

¹/₂ cup Dijon mustard

2 tablespoons Cheater Rub de la Maison (page 47)

Serve the pork in lamb's clothing with couscous, rice, garlicky white beans, tomatoes and fresh basil, Greek feta salad, pita bread, or anything inspired by any country that touches the Mediterranean—and anything other than sweet barbecue beans and traditional slaw.

HEAT the oven to 350°F.

CUT the ribs into 2- to 3-bone sections with a sharp knife. Place them in a large roasting pan.

COMBINE the mustard and the dry rub in a small bowl and stir to form a paste. Spread the paste all over the ribs, coating them evenly.

ROAST the ribs, uncovered, for about 1 hour. They should look well browned and the meat should be tender.

All-Day Crock Dogs
in Smoky Beer Broth

*L*ong *ago R. B. learned that grilling hot dogs and sausages isn't as low-stress or as simple as it sounds. He's still recovering from childhood campfire hot dogs that turned out more like bike inner tubes. R. B.'s current recovery program requires him to just let it all go. He tries not to be an annoying guest at casual barbecues or hover nervously near the grill when a distracted host leaves his post.*

MAKES 12 SERVINGS

Two 12-ounce beers

2 bay leaves

1 medium onion, sliced

$1/4$ cup bottled smoke

2 pounds hot dogs

Dogs on a grill need to be watched or they'll quickly run away from you. When done right they get a light char and a bite that pops. Since game day is supposed to be about the game and the guests, get the dogs done before the national anthem. The key to dogs lasting well into the postgame commentary is the slow cooker.

Before the game, grill, broil, or pan-char your sausages—brats, knacks, red hots, kielbasa, smoked turkey and chicken sausages, even those basil–sun-dried tomato–mango brands. Keep them warm in spiked hot dog "water."

Use the recipe as a guideline. A large slow cooker can easily keep 5 or 6 pounds of dogs in a hot steamy bath. Just use enough liquid to keep the dogs partially but comfortably submerged, adding more water if needed. Once heated through, the links will be ready as long as the cooker is plugged in.

And if the slow cooker is tied up with your famous chili or nacho dip, put a heavy-bottomed covered pot over low heat on the stove. Otherwise, grab an extension cord, set the slow cooker on the coffee table, and you won't even have to leave your seat.

COMBINE the beer, bay leaves, onion, and bottled smoke in a medium to large slow cooker (at least 4 quarts). Turn on high to heat the broth.

Lightly **CHAR** the hot dogs at a moderate heat level using a broiler, grill pan, skillet, toaster oven, or grill.

ADD the hot dogs to the slow cooker. Cover and reduce the heat to low. Add beer or water and additional dogs as necessary.   *(continued)*

VARIATION

You can cook hot dogs in a covered dry slow cooker. The hot chamber will give the dogs a charred look and feel, and you don't have to watch them every minute. Sprinkle in a little bottled smoke, if you like. Cook them on high for about an hour or on low for two. They will dry out and shrivel up if left in the cooker too long. For all-day serving, go with the Smoky Beer Broth.

CROCK DOG FEST ESSENTIALS

Even wieners deserve a little respect. A little prep, some care, and occasional site policing are all it takes. If you take your dogs seriously, everyone else will, too. There's no magic, just attention to detail and quality.

1. *Get plenty of wieners for everyone. Three varieties will keep people interested and talking about the food. Figure at least two dogs per hungry adult.*
2. *For smaller appetites and kids, slice some dogs into 2-inch pieces and serve with toothpicks or wooden skewers.*
3. *Min loves a mustard tasting and is forever adding new ones to the fridge door condiment collection. Go with an odd number, always at room temperature, and arrange them like you mean it. Tasting note cards are a plus for those not so focused on the game.*
4. *Display all condiments—including ketchup, barbecue sauce, relishes, onions, pickles, and peppers—in bowls with serving spoons, placed for easy access. Keep it tidy.*
5. *Like quality condiments, buns count. They need to be fresh, easy to separate, and not presmashed by the car door. Take them out of the wrapper and serve them under a cloth in a basket. We also love the Texas trick of dogs in warm tortillas.*

A few other tips from R. B., the party Eagle Scout:
- *Serve chips in large bowls, not out of the bag.*
- *Stock a couple of good-size coolers with plenty of ice and beverages for easy self-serve. Always overestimate your ice needs. Remember, ice melts.*
- *Splurge on sturdy plastic cutlery, plates, and napkins corralled together and ready to go.*
- *Provide good plastic drink cups and a couple of permanent markers for efficient cup ID management.*

CHEATER BBQ

Wiener Burgers with Main Dog Slaw

Just as one special cocktail sets the party mood, one special condiment streamlines the party food. Try Min's Main Dog Slaw as a simple solution to the cluttered condiment bar or mustard tasting. The switch from hot dog to hamburger bun puts a signature twist on a dog.

COMBINE all the slaw ingredients in a medium bowl. Blend well, cover, and refrigerate until serving time.

HEAT the broiler. Slice the bratwursts lengthwise until almost cut through. Place on a baking sheet.

BROIL the brats about 4 inches from the heat source until seared on both sides and warmed throughout. (You can also brown the brats in a skillet over medium heat.)

TOP with the cheese (if you like) and broil (or cover the skillet) and cook an additional minute until the cheese melts.

PLACE a wiener on each bun and pile on the slaw.

....
MAKES 6 SERVINGS

For the Main Dog Slaw
2 cups slaw mix
$^1/_2$ cup chopped red onion
$^1/_2$ cup sweet pickle relish
$^1/_4$ cup spicy brown mustard
1 tablespoon sugar
$^1/_2$ teaspoon celery salt
Dash of hot pepper sauce

For the Wiener Burgers
6 short, fat, fully cooked
   bratwursts or other hot dogs
6 slices Swiss cheese (optional)
6 hamburger buns

Hot Dog Reuben Wraps

Min fell for tortilla-wrapped dogs outside of Austin, Texas, years ago after a meal of wrapped barbecued sausages. The Texas hill country is a barbecue melting pot, thanks to the influences of German settlers and our Mexican neighbors. Since then, Min has pretty much sworn off hot dog buns. With a chronically overcrowded kitchen and a jammed freezer, a pack of tortillas stays out of the way, doesn't get mashed up, and offers a lot more options. The kids don't miss the buns one bit either.

MAKES 6 SERVINGS

6 slices Swiss cheese, cut into thin strips

About 1 cup warm sauerkraut

6 Crock Dogs (page 71)

About ½ cup Fridge Door Special Sauce (page 125)

Pickled jalapeño slices

Six 8-inch flour tortillas, warmed

PLACE a few strips of cheese, a little sauerkraut, a hot dog, a spoonful of special sauce, and jalapeños to taste on a warm tortilla. Wrap, repeat, and eat.

Cheater Smoked Chubb Bologna

If you're feeling that cooking has gotten way too complicated, try smoking a big chubb bologna in the slow cooker. It might just be one of the best tasting, most underwrought meats around. Believe it or not, smoked chubb bologna has become a menu regular in barbecue joints. This fun, affordable, already-cooked sausage quickly picks up smoke in an outdoor smoker or in a slow cooker.

Think of the possibilities. Give the brats a break and boost tailgating team spirit with a load of bologna patty melts oozing with cheese and grilled onions. Lighten the mood with cracker chubb mini bologna burgers. How about teriyaki-glazed bologna with pineapple chunks in lettuce cups?

MAKES 10 TO 12 SERVINGS

One 3-pound big chubb bologna, cut into $1/2$- to 1-inch slices

2 tablespoons bottled smoke

PLACE the bologna slices in a slow cooker and pour the bottled smoke over them.

COVER and cook on high for 2 to 3 hours or on low for 4 to 5 hours.

ASK your doctor if Cheater Smoked Chubb Bologna is right for you. Serve as directed.

Chubb Patty Melt

SERVE chubb bologna slices with melted Cheddar and sautéed onions on rye.

Philly Cheese Chubb

STUFF chubb bologna slices in a crusty sub roll with cheese sauce and sautéed peppers and onions.

....
Barbecue Slaw Chubb

BRUSH chubb bologna slices with barbecue sauce and serve on buns with mustardy slaw.

....
Chipotle Chubb Burger

TRY chubb bologna with melted pepper Jack cheese, lettuce, and fresh tomato, slathered with a blend of chipotle pepper sauce and mayo.

....
Asian Chubb Lettuce Wraps

TOSS chunks of chubb bologna with teriyaki sauce and pineapple chunks. Wrap in lettuce cups.

....
Cracker Chubb Mini Burgers

FILL soft dinner rolls with chubb bologna, your choice of melted cheese, and a pickle slice. (Cracker chubb is the smaller bologna; the rounds fit on crackers.)

Cheater Brines

Brine is a salty solution that infuses moisture and flavor into pork, chicken, and turkey, especially lean cuts like breast and loin that tend toward dryness under high heat.

Our basic rule of thumb is 1 cup of kosher salt per gallon of water. When we add sugar to a brine, we use half as much sugar as salt. Turkey can take a little sugar, but we tend to omit it for chicken. Make as much brine as you need to submerge the meat comfortably. The 2-cup amounts below are suitable for 2 pounds of meat. Double the recipe for up to 5 pounds of meat. For large cuts like a whole turkey or a big pork loin, mix the brine in a clean cooler, add the meat, and top with bags of ice to keep it cold.

Pork especially takes to sweet-flavored brines just like it does to sweet sauces and rubs. Off-the-shelf sweet liquids like apple cider, lemonade, and sweet tea need just some salt and smoke to turn into easy brines. A plastic bag and an hour in the fridge, and you'll never think twice about not brining again. Small cuts of meat need less brining. An hour is fine for pork chops and chicken parts, while a whole turkey can go overnight.

Basic Smoky Brine

2 tablespoons kosher salt
1 tablespoon sugar
1/4 cup bottled smoke

COMBINE the ingredients with 2 cups water in a sealable plastic bag set in a bowl.

Apple Cider Brine

2 cups apple cider
2 tablespoons kosher salt
1/4 cup bottled smoke

COMBINE the ingredients in a sealable plastic bag set in a bowl.

Limeade or Lemonade Brine

2 cups limeade or lemonade
2 tablespoons kosher salt
$\frac{1}{4}$ cup bottled smoke

COMBINE all the ingredients in a sealable plastic bag set in a bowl.

Sweet Tea Brine

2 cups sweet brewed tea
2 tablespoons kosher salt
$\frac{1}{4}$ cup bottled smoke

COMBINE all the ingredients in a sealable plastic bag set in a bowl.

Cider-Soy Pork Tenderloin

No, even we can't live only on pulled pork barbecue. Now that we've taken you through the fat trenches with delicious pulled pork aplenty, here's sensible lean tenderloin that's quick to brine and broil. Don't overcook it, or it will taste like sensible shoes. Take the flavor in any direction with your choice of dry rub.

The cider-soy brine is essential for keeping the "tender" in the ultralean tenderloin and adds a nice penetrating flavor that's impossible to get with a quick topical seasoning. Change up the brine to keep things interesting. Any of the brines on pages 77 to 78 will perform the same juicy service.

MAKES 6 SERVINGS

For the brine

2 cups apple cider

$\frac{1}{2}$ cup soy sauce

$\frac{1}{4}$ cup bottled smoke

1 tablespoon kosher salt

One 2-pound pork tenderloin

Vegetable oil

1 tablespoon cheater dry rub (you pick, pages 45 to 47)

COMBINE all the brine ingredients in a large sealable plastic bag set in a bowl.

ADD the tenderloin. Seal the bag and massage it gently to blend the ingredients. Refrigerate the tenderloin for 1 to 4 hours.

REMOVE the tenderloin from the brine and discard the liquid. Rinse the tenderloin, pat dry, and place on a rimmed baking sheet. Heat the broiler.

COAT all sides of the tenderloin lightly with vegetable oil and sprinkle with the dry rub.

BROIL the tenderloin about 4 inches from the heat source for 20 minutes, turning once during broiling. Test for doneness. The internal temperature should be 150°F to 160°F.

Ultimate Cheater Pork Loin

A pork loin is a roast of uncut pork loin chops. Leaner than pork shoulder and cheaper than pork tenderloin, it's a popular cut for grilling and slicing to feed a crowd. It's also perfect for any one of our Cheater Brines (pages 77 to 78).

Our cheater meat slicer is a compact electric knife—the affordable, no-frills, unsung hero of kitchen appliances. R. B. calls it the indoor chain saw. Ultimate Cheater Pork Loin sliced paper-thin will make a pile of Cuban Fingers (page 176).

MAKES 6 TO 8 SERVINGS

1 batch of brine (you pick)

One 3-pound pork loin

Vegetable oil

**2 tablespoons Cheater Basic
    Dry Rub (page 45)**

BRINE the loin for 4 to 6 hours in the refrigerator (see page 77).

HEAT the oven to 500°F.

DRAIN the loin, discarding the brine. Rinse and pat dry. Place the loin in a large roasting pan and brush with a light coating of vegetable oil. Sprinkle all sides of the loin with the dry rub.

PLACE the loin in the oven and immediately reduce the heat to 300°F. Cook for 1 hour, or until a meat thermometer reaches 155°F. Let rest for 10 to 15 minutes before slicing.

Steakhouse Pork Chops

Do you suffer the old internal temperature anxiety around pork chops? When is pork really done? Is it safe?

The other white meat should really be the pale pink meat because once it goes white, it's too late for anything but lots of gravy. The pork guys say 160°F (and that's a lot lower than they used to say). The restaurant guys say pull pork out of the heat at 135°F. We tend to go with 140°F, and it seems to work.

To tame the chewy chops, you should brine first. Then be bold enough to stay in the pink. Once out of the brine, the chops must be patted dry or you won't get any crust. Wet chops look steamed. For the restaurant hot salamander sear, give lean pork chops a little oil massage to encourage browning under a hot broiler.

MAKES 4 SERVINGS

4 bone-in pork chops about 1 inch thick (about 3 pounds)

1 batch of brine (you pick, pages 77 to 78)

Vegetable oil

4 teaspoons cheater dry rub (you pick, pages 45 to 47)

BRINE the chops for 1 hour in the refrigerator.

DRAIN the chops, discarding the brine. Rinse and pat dry.

HEAT the broiler. Place the chops on a baking sheet or broiler pan. Coat both sides of the meat lightly with oil. Sprinkle the dry rub on both sides of the meat, using 1 teaspoon per chop.

BROIL the chops about 4 inches from the heat source for 8 to 10 minutes per side. The internal temperature should be 140°F to 150°F when you remove them from the oven. The temperature will rise another 5 to 10 degrees while the chops rest before serving.

CHAPTER 4

Cheater Poultry

CHICKEN CHEAT SHEET

We're puzzled by America's cultural obsession with breasts. Thirty years ago when flavor still counted and chicken parts came with skin and bones, legs outsold breasts. Since the '80s, we've been implanted with a fat phobia that's pushed us into the open arms of enlarged chicken breast meat. In fact, nearly all of the eighty-plus pounds of chicken we each eat every year is the boneless, skinless breast kind. Americans prefer it two-to-one over dark meat. While we're consuming all the dry breast meat we can, the rest of the world is enjoying our exported legs and thighs.

Boneless, skinless chicken breasts are tempting. They look great, they're easy to handle, and they're versatile. They're also bland and hard to keep juicy. We use chicken breasts, but limit them to poaching and hobo crock cooking. They're fine, but not our favorite part of the chicken.

While you can substitute breast meat in the recipes, we urge you to reconsider legs and thighs. The higher fat content in the "pork butt" of chicken makes them much better at absorbing smoke. The chicken industry has undressed dark meat by conveniently removing the bones and skin to coax us all back to thighs. Thankfully, they still can't grow a chicken without legs, so dark meat is a delicious bargain, sometimes at about half the price.

Ultimate Cheater Pulled Chicken

A crock of pulled smoked chicken is the original white meat's answer to pulled pork. And because it's chicken, it has endless uses in sandwiches, casseroles, soups and stews, tacos, and burritos. The key is having the chicken cooked, pulled, and ready to go; then you can bid farewell to that dried-out supermarket rotisserie bird.

An hour in a simple saltwater brine adds moisture and freshens up the bird. We limit brining time for smaller cuts like chicken pieces and pork chops to an hour to keep the salt flavor under control. When we brine for longer periods, we usually go lighter on the dry rub or switch to Cheater No-Salt Dry Rub (page 47).

To us, the best pulled chicken is all dark meat or a light and dark meat combination. If you use breast meat only, the meat will be stringier and noticeably drier. There's nothing you can do about it except brine first and add sauce at the end.

MAKES 8 SERVINGS

5 pounds chicken parts—pick-of-the-chick pack, leg/thigh quarters, breasts, or a combination, trimmed of excess skin and fat

For the simple brine

1/4 cup kosher salt

2 tablespoons sugar

2 tablespoons cheater dry rub (you pick, pages 45 to 47)

1/2 cup bottled smoke

To brine the chicken, **PLACE** it in an extra-large 2-gallon sealable plastic bag set in a large bowl.

POUR the salt and sugar into a 1-quart plastic bottle with a tight-fitting lid. Add 3 cups of cold water. Cover tightly and shake vigourously to dissolve the salt and sugar.

POUR the brine over the chicken. Seal the bag and blend by gently massaging the bag. Refrigerate for 1 hour.

Just before cooking, **DRAIN** the chicken, discarding the brine. Rinse the chicken under cold water and pat dry. Place in a large slow cooker (at least 5 quarts), sprinkle with the dry rub, and add the bottled smoke. Cover and cook on high for 4 to 6 hours or on low for 8 to 10 hours.

REMOVE the chicken. When cool enough to handle, remove the bones and skin. Shred the meat with your fingers. Use in your favorite Two-Timing Cheater chicken recipes (see chapter 8).

Cheater Super Pollo

Super Pollo is a hybrid Mexican-American barbecue chicken restaurant in Nashville that combines Tennessee hickory smoke with chili-rubbed chicken, corn tortillas, and fresh salsas. *Unlike the more traditional barbecue shack approach where chicken doused in sweet sauce plays second fiddle to pulled pork, ribs, and brisket, here the cumin-and-chili-rubbed chicken is the star. Handmade corn tortillas replace the usual corn cakes, and rich soupy pintos replace the standard sweet barbecue baked beans. We smoky-brine our Super Pollo first and spice it up with Cheater Chili Dry Rub. Serve with tortillas, pintos, rice, and plenty of salsa and pickled jalapeños.*

....

MAKES 4 TO 6 SERVINGS

6 pounds chicken leg/thigh quarters and breast quarters, trimmed of excess skin and fat

For the smoky brine

1/2 cup kosher salt

1/4 cup sugar

1/2 cup bottled smoke

1/4 cup Cheater Chili Dry Rub (page 45)

To brine the chicken, **PLACE** it in an extra-large 2-gallon sealable plastic bag set in a large bowl.

POUR the salt and sugar into a 1-quart plastic bottle with a tight-fitting lid. Add 3 cups of cold water. Cover tightly and shake vigorously to dissolve the salt and sugar.

POUR the brine over the chicken and add 5 cups of cold water and the bottled smoke. Seal the bag and blend by gently massaging the bag.

REFRIGERATE the chicken for 1 hour. Drain and rinse, discarding the brine. Pat dry.

HEAT the oven to 325°F. Place the chicken on a large rimmed baking sheet and rub on all sides with the dry rub. Cook for 1 1/2 hours or until fork-tender.

Chicksticks

Frying chicken is like outdoor barbecue: Sometimes we just don't have the energy to do the work. In a pinch, chicksticks make a nice pile of crispy chicken strips with a high crust-to-bite ratio. Our trick is to roll the chicken breast strips in a mix of oil and bottled smoke before breading. Serve them hot or cold and take them anywhere. Kids love them with ketchup and honey mustard; sports fans drag them through buffalo sauce or chipotle ketchup (see Note). Cut them up to top a Caesar salad. Load them in a hoagie roll with pickles, mayo, and lettuce. For fancier meals, serve them with fresh lemon.

MAKES 6 TO 8 SERVINGS

2 pounds boneless, skinless chicken breast halves or chicken tenders

1/4 cup peanut or vegetable oil

2 tablespoons bottled smoke

1 cup regular or panko bread crumbs

2 tablespoons Cheater Basic Dry Rub (page 45)

HEAT the oven to 450°F. Lightly coat a large rimmed baking sheet with nonstick cooking spray.

CUT each chicken breast half into 4 to 5 long, thin strips. (If you're using chicken tenders, they don't need to be cut up.)

COMBINE the chicken, oil, and bottled smoke in a large bowl. Toss to coat the chicken evenly.

COMBINE the bread crumbs and dry rub in a shallow bowl and blend well. Coat each chicken piece in the breading and place it on the baking sheet. Do not crowd the pieces. Use two medium pans, if necessary.

BAKE for 10 minutes. Remove the chicken from the oven and heat the broiler. Broil the chicken about 4 inches from the heat source until it is crisp and nicely browned, 3 to 5 minutes.

Note: For a quick cheater chipotle ketchup, combine 1 cup ketchup with 1 to 2 tablespoons chopped chipotle peppers in adobo sauce.

Smoke-Poached Chicken Breasts

Poaching sounds chef-toque complicated, but simmering meat in a liquid on the stovetop is pretty straightforward and keeps the kitchen cooler in hot weather. Better yet, poaching is especially good for keeping the usually dry chicken breast meat moist. We even add a smoky component to the poaching liquid for terrific smoked chicken salads and sandwiches.

For chicken salad, aim for a balance of smoke, sweet, and savory. The smoke really takes to fresh and dried fruits like green apple, pineapple, mango or papaya, raisins, dried cherries, or cranberries. Parsley and green onion are always a good choice, and celery and good mayonnaise are a must.

MAKES 3 TO 4 CUPS

One 14-ounce can chicken broth

1/4 cup bottled smoke

2 celery ribs, cut into 2-inch pieces

1 medium onion, sliced into thin wedges

1 bay leaf

4 boneless, skinless chicken breast halves (about 2 pounds)

COMBINE the chicken broth, 3 cups water, the bottled smoke, celery, onion, and bay leaf in a large skillet with straight sides.

BRING the broth to a low boil over high heat. Reduce the heat to medium-low. Carefully add the chicken. Simmer for 20 to 25 minutes, partially covered, until the internal temperature reaches 160°F.

REMOVE the chicken and discard the poaching liquid.

Hot Pot Chicken

A superhot oven is what separates the professionals from the rest of us. While we dream of 900°F, we're making the most of our enamel-coated cast-iron Dutch oven in 500°F. Chicken cooked in a hot covered pot cheats your way to moist meat and crisp dry-rubbed salty skin just like the pros.

Whole chickens are easy to cut in half with poultry shears, a sharp knife, or a cleaver, or have your meat guy do it. First, get the pot raging hot. Start the chicken halves skin side down to sear in the juices. Flip halfway through cooking and leave the cover off to crisp the skin. Good pot holders and tongs are a must. Skip the sauce because the skin is killer good.

MAKES 2 TO 4 SERVINGS

One 3- to 4-pound chicken, cut in half

2 tablespoons cheater dry rub (you pick, pages 45 to 47)

1 tablespoon vegetable oil

PLACE a 7-quart enamel-coated cast-iron pot with a tight-fitting lid in the oven. Heat the oven to 500°F and let the pot get good and hot, about 15 minutes.

Meanwhile, RINSE the chicken halves and pat them dry. Sprinkle all sides with the dry rub.

Carefully PULL out the oven rack that's holding the hot pot and remove the cover. Pour in the oil and place the chicken halves skin side down in the pot. Quickly cover the pot and close the oven. Bake for 30 minutes.

REMOVE the cover, carefully flip the chicken halves to skin side up, and bake uncovered for 15 to 20 minutes, until the chicken reaches an internal temperature of 175°F in the thick part of the dark leg/thigh meat.

Hobo Crock Whole Smoked Chicken

*T*he hobo crock method was inspired by R. B.'s Boy Scout campout foil hobo-pack cuisine. Cheater hobo crock meats take advantage of this simple method for infusing foods with flavor and trapping moisture. Meats are tightly wrapped with seasonings and bottled smoke and placed in a slow cooker. The cool thing is that you won't open the pack to find a pile of soggy skin and bones, as you might expect. The chicken maintains its structure, browns on top, and can be carved and sliced. This method will also successfully tame a beef brisket (page 113).

Indoors or out, the only issue we have is over the grade of aluminum foil for wrapping the bird. R. B. requires heavy duty—one of those barbecue guy things. Min uses the thinner, everyday stuff because she knows that the juices are going to leak into the crock anyway, so who cares whether the cheaper foil springs a hole or two.

....
MAKES 2 TO 4 SERVINGS

One 4- to 5-pound chicken

3 tablespoons Cheater Basic
   Dry Rub (page 45)

1 onion, quartered

¼ cup bottled smoke

LINE a large slow cooker (at least 5 quarts) with a sheet of heavy-duty aluminum foil large enough to completely wrap around the chicken.

PLACE the chicken in the slow cooker and generously coat all sides as well as the cavity with the dry rub. Place the onion in the cavity. Pour the bottled smoke over the chicken.

FOLD the foil around the chicken for a snug fit and cover. Cook on high for 3 to 4 hours or on low for 5 to 6 hours, until the chicken is pull-apart tender and reaches an internal temperature of at least 175°F in the thick part of the dark leg/thigh meat.

Carefully LIFT the chicken out of the crock. Let it rest for 10 minutes. Discard the onion and carve.

Hobo Crock Chicken Breasts with Bacon

*L*et's face it, everything tastes better with bacon, especially chicken breasts in need of a little fat and flavor. You know by now that the boneless, skinless chicken breast is not our top choice, but with a little rub, some smoke, and slow, moist cooking these breasts are okay and ready for casseroles, soups, and sandwiches. Skip the bacon if you're on a fat-restricted diet.

MAKES 6 TO 8 SERVINGS

3 pounds boneless, skinless chicken breast halves (about 6)

3 tablespoons cheater dry rub (you pick, pages 45 to 47)

1/2 pound bacon or a chunk of salt pork

1/4 cup bottled smoke

LINE a large slow cooker (at least 5 quarts) with a sheet of heavy-duty aluminum foil large enough to completely wrap around the chicken.

PLACE half the chicken in the slow cooker and generously coat all sides with half the dry rub. Add the remaining chicken and coat evenly with the remaining dry rub. Sprinkle the bacon over the top. Pour the bottled smoke over the chicken.

FOLD the foil around the chicken for a snug fit and cover. Cook on high for 3 to 4 hours or on low for 5 to 6 hours, until the chicken is pull-apart tender and reaches an internal temperature of 160°F. Discard the bacon.

Gunsmoke Chicken

Grilled chicken marinated in Worcestershire and soy sauce was one of the first things R. B.'s Gourmet-subscribing mother, Loie, taught him to cook. It was probably the first marinade he'd ever tasted, and he loved the way it quickly permeated the chicken skin with color and the meat with salty flavor. Later on, he discovered that Loie's salty black concoction is a common barbecue trick available at the supermarket under several labels. Both the popular store blends and Loie's homemade pack quite a punch and don't need much time to work up some flavor on chicken or beef.

Here is Loie's cheater recipe, which you can easily double and store in a sealed container in the fridge. Use it for chicken or a Gunsmoke steak cooked on the grill, in a skillet, or under the broiler.

....

MAKES 4 SERVINGS

1/2 cup Worcestershire sauce

1/4 cup soy sauce

1/4 cup bottled smoke

3 pounds chicken pieces, trimmed of excess skin and fat

COMBINE the Worcestershire sauce, soy sauce, and bottled smoke in a large sealable plastic bag set in a bowl.

ADD the chicken. Seal the bag and massage the bag to coat the pieces. Refrigerate for 1 to 2 hours.

HEAT the oven to 500°F. Remove the chicken from the bag and place it in a roasting pan or on a rimmed baking sheet. Discard the marinade.

PUT the chicken in the oven and immediately reduce the temperature to 350°F. Bake for 1 1/2 hours for very tender, fall-off-the-bone chicken. Reduce the baking time to 1 hour for chicken breasts.

Asian Honey-Lacquered BBQ Chicken

C heating doesn't mean just opening a bottle. As our provider of primo Tennessee hardwood and traveling philosopher, Jerry Elston, likes to remind us, sometimes you can't get out of doing the work. Like most bottled barbecue sauces, Asian-style sauces are cheater easy and get the point across. But usually they taste overly sweet and empty, with little going for them besides sugar and soy. Here's a brush-on honey lacquer for dry-rubbed chicken with real Asian flavor using pantry staples and some freshly grated ginger.

PREHEAT the oven to 500°F.

PLACE the chicken in a roasting pan or on a rimmed baking sheet. Sprinkle the dry rub on all sides.

PLACE the chicken in the oven and immediately reduce the temperature to 400°F. Roast for 30 minutes.

While the chicken bakes, **COMBINE** all the ingredients for the Honey Lacquer in a small bowl.

REMOVE the chicken from the oven and brush with the Honey Lacquer. Return the chicken to the oven and roast for 10 minutes, until the lacquer sets. Sprinkle with sesame seeds.

MAKES 4 TO 6 SERVINGS

3 pounds chicken leg/thigh quarters (about 4), trimmed of excess skin and fat

2 tablespoons Cheater Basic Dry Rub (page 45)

For the Honey Lacquer

1/4 cup honey

1 tablespoon soy sauce

1 tablespoon ketchup

1 garlic clove, minced

1 tablespoon grated fresh ginger

1 tablespoon rice vinegar

1 teaspoon dry mustard

2 tablespoons sesame seeds, toasted (see page 67)

Filipino Adobo-Q Chicken

Adobo is a Filipino obsession like barbecue is in America. The key is slow cooking in a mix of Filipino sugarcane vinegar and soy sauce. We think it has a sour-salty vibe similar to American vinegar barbecue sauces. Filipino sugarcane vinegar is soft and mild, more like Asian rice vinegar than cider vinegar. We stumbled on it at the international market along with Filipino soy sauce. If it's in Nashville, it's probably available in most cities in the United States.

Not to be confused with Mexican canned chipotle peppers in adobo sauce, this Filipino adobo is a simmering pot of chicken in a tart, salty bath of what probably looks like too much vinegar and soy sauce. You can crisp the chicken on the grill or under the broiler after cooking. Sometimes we use the slow cooker for a pile of soft pulled adobo chicken. Leave out the water and cook the chicken on high for three to four hours. You can also cook beef short ribs or pork butt in the same mix. Whatever the meat or the method, serve it with plenty of white rice.

MAKES 6 TO 8 SERVINGS

4 pounds chicken leg/thigh quarters (about 6), trimmed of excess skin and fat

1 cup soy sauce, preferably Filipino soy sauce

1 cup Filipino sugarcane vinegar or rice vinegar

6 garlic cloves, crushed and coarsely chopped

2 bay leaves

1 serrano chile, sliced (optional)

1 teaspoon black pepper

COMBINE all the ingredients in a large pot. Bring to a boil, cover, and simmer for 30 minutes, turning the chicken once or twice.

REMOVE the chicken from the liquid and set aside. Simmer the sauce gently until reduced to about 1 cup. Heat the broiler.

BROIL (or grill if you feel like it) the chicken about 5 minutes a side until the skin is brown and crisp. Serve the chicken with the adobo sauce and white rice.

Bar-B-Cuban Chicken

One of our top five cheater recipes was inspired by a summer cookout at the Nashville hideout of songwriter/producer Desmond Child, the genius behind scores of hit songs, including "Dude Looks Like a Lady," "Livin' on a Prayer," and "Livin' La Vida Loca."

Margarita, a member of Desmond's Miami posse, is an excellent cook and veteran cheater. The chart-topping single of the incredible Cuban feast was Bar-B-Cuban Chicken. After marinating chicken legs and thighs overnight, she cheated big-time by cooking them in the oven before the party. In a matter of minutes, the precooked chicken was effortlessly seared on the grill in a showy haze before a live audience.

Garlic and tangy lemon not only filled the air, they had penetrated deep into the meat (and our clothes). Margarita admitted, "I don't measure and I always use too much garlic. I say, it's good? No. More."

"How much garlic do you use, Margarita?"

"Too much," she said.

This is our cover of Margarita's smash hit.

MAKES 6 TO 8 SERVINGS

4 pounds chicken legs and thighs, trimmed of excess skin and fat

1 cup fresh lemon juice

$1/3$ cup olive oil

12 garlic cloves, minced

1 chicken bouillon cube, crumbled

2 teaspoons kosher salt

Handful of chopped fresh rosemary and oregano

Black pepper

PLACE the chicken in a large sealable plastic bag. Add the remaining ingredients, seal the bag, and massage to blend the ingredients. Refrigerate overnight for maximum impact.

REMOVE the chicken from the marinade. Place the chicken in a roasting pan and toss it with a little of the marinade; discard the rest. Bake at 350°F for 40 minutes.

REMOVE the chicken from the oven and finish it on the grill or under the broiler about 4 inches from the heat source, turning frequently, until the skin is nicely charred and crisp and you can smell the garlic down the street.

Tandoori BBQ Chicken Thighs

One hot Tennessee evening Min's neighbor, Raj Kumar, handed R. B. a green coconut and a cleaver and said, "Chop the top off that thing. Let's have a drink."

We love Raj. Dinner at his kitchen table is part spiritual recharge, part therapy, part comedy hour. Even better, Raj knows how to cook.

MAKES 6 TO 8 SERVINGS

4 pounds skinless chicken thighs (about 8 thighs)

2 cups buttermilk (optional)

2 to 3 tablespoons Cheater Indian Rub (page 46)

2 large onions, cut into rings

2 lemons, cut into wedges

After one question too many from us, he took us to Apna Bazaar, Nashville's Costco of Indian provisions. Soon every dish we made required two kinds of cardamom pods, a chunk of cinnamon bark, cumin and coriander seeds, mango pickles, and a chutney or two on the side. Raj kindly indulged us in our enthusiasm and, in time, our spicing acquired some much-needed subtlety. As Raj advised, one should wonder about flavor, not be hit over the head with it.

Tandoori BBQ Chicken Thighs use bone-in, skinless dark meat typical of Indian cuisine and our balanced dry rub approach, accented with either a simple curry

GREEN COCONUT COCKTAIL

Raj had his first fresh coconut cocktail in Brazil while serving in the Merchant Marines as a young man. It's still one of his special-occasion drinks and well suited for a tropical evening on the deck. Use fresh white coconuts, not the hard dark brown ones, and chill them first. Plastic-wrapped fresh white coconuts have had the heavy green husk removed. We run into them at international markets and occasionally among the specialty produce at the regular supermarket.

To mix this drink, very carefully make a small hole in the top with a cleaver or heavy knife. Insert a straw and drink some of the coconut milk to make room for the liquor. Pour in vodka, rum, bourbon, or Scotch and stir it up with the straw. When all you hear are sucking sounds, crack open the shell and feast on the soft white coconut flesh inside.

powder or garam masala, both readily available spices. Add cayenne pepper for more bite. When time allows, we adhere to the tandoori tradition of soaking the chicken in plain yogurt before seasoning the meat. In 900°F tandoori ovens, the yogurt ensures moist chicken, and it's just as worthwhile at home. We often substitute buttermilk for the yogurt because it's cheaper and coats the meat instantly.

RINSE the chicken thighs and trim of excess fat. If marinating, combine the chicken and buttermilk in a large bowl or sealable plastic bag. Cover or seal and refrigerate for 1 to 8 hours.

HEAT the oven to 450°F.

PLACE the chicken on a large rimmed baking sheet and sprinkle all sides with the dry rub. Bake for 30 minutes.

TOSS the onion rings over the chicken and bake for an additional 5 to 10 minutes, until the onions are slightly soft and the internal temperature of the chicken is 170°F. Serve with the lemon.

Jamaican Jerked Drums

About fifteen years ago R. B. thought his next-door neighbor, who was out grilling some chicken, called him a jerk. Back then, R. B. hadn't heard of jerk seasoning, and his neighbor seemed like a nice, quiet fellow who pretty much kept to himself. When R. B. turned down the Bob Marley, everything got straightened out, and the chicken was delicious.

A jerk dry rub requires allspice, thyme, and some heat. The Scotch bonnet pepper is the traditional choice, but that's too many Scoville heat units for us. We keep the heat out of the rub, then sprinkle on cayenne to customize the chicken to suit everyone.

MAKES 6 TO 8 SERVINGS

4 pounds chicken drumsticks (about 12)

¼ cup vegetable oil

4 tablespoons Cheater Jamaican Jerk Rub (page 46)

Cayenne pepper to taste

Lime wedges

HEAT the oven to 450°F.

PLACE the drumsticks on a large rimmed baking sheet. Drizzle with the oil, coating the skin until it's shiny. Sprinkle all sides of the drumsticks with 3 tablespoons of the dry rub. Roast for 20 minutes.

REMOVE the drumsticks from the oven and turn them over with tongs. Sprinkle with the remaining tablespoon of dry rub and cayenne to taste for spicier drums.

ROAST for an additional 20 minutes. Serve with fresh lime wedges.

Hobo Crock Turkey Breast

The best part of Thanksgiving weekend might be a postholiday turkey sandwich when the guests are gone and you're hanging out at home. When you don't get that sandwich (because somebody wrapped up all the turkey to go home with somebody's cousin), it can haunt you.

No need to wait another year and another holiday. No need to cook a whole turkey, either. Like Hobo Crock Whole Smoked Chicken (page 90), a whole turkey breast does really well wrapped in foil and cooked in a slow cooker. You can even pull off a handsome skin with melted butter mixed with bottled smoke. If you buy a frozen breast, remember to give it a few days in the fridge to thaw completely before cooking.

MAKES 12 SERVINGS

One 5- to 6-pound turkey breast

2 to 3 tablespoons Cheater Basic Dry Rub (page 45)

1 onion, quartered

4 tablespoons ($^{1}/_{2}$ stick) butter, melted

$^{1}/_{4}$ cup bottled smoke

LINE a large slow cooker (at least 5 quarts) with a sheet of heavy-duty aluminum foil large enough to completely wrap around the turkey breast.

PLACE the turkey breast in the slow cooker and generously coat all sides as well as the cavity with the dry rub. Tuck the onion in the breast cavity.

COMBINE the butter and bottled smoke and pour the mixture over the breast.

FOLD the foil around the turkey for a snug fit and cover. Cook on high for 5 to 6 hours or on low for 8 to 10 hours, until the turkey reaches an internal temperature of at least 160°F.

Carefully LIFT the turkey out of the crock. Discard the onion and carve.

CHEATER POULTRY

Smoked Whole Turkey in a Bag

One ambitious Thanksgiving eve we gathered family, friends, and neighbors over to the house and deep-fried all their turkeys for the next day. That was fun and exhausting. Of course, keeping with R. B.'s former motto "If it's worth doing, it's worth overdoing," we finished the turkey fry with a big batch of catfish. At least we got our money's worth out of the peanut oil.

For other ambitious Thanksgivings, R. B. has stayed up all night (by himself) nursing Tom Turkey's fire with a formula of wet hickory chips and Tennessee whiskey. Those were the memorable years when R. B. dozed through Thanksgiving dinner and got along particularly well with everyone.

Now that R. B. is in cheater recovery, a wet-smoked turkey in an oven bag leaves him with the single challenge of keeping things light and deferential at the dinner table.

The cheater turkey is always moist, tender, and smoky and shows off a golden brown sheen.

MAKES 8 SERVINGS

For the smoke brine (double or triple as necessary)

1 1/2 cups kosher salt

3/4 cup sugar

2 cups bottled smoke

For the turkey

One 12-pound fresh or fully thawed turkey (not kosher)

2 to 3 tablespoons Cheater No-Salt Dry Rub (page 47)

Dried oregano, sage, marjoram, and thyme

3 celery ribs, cut into 2- to 3-inch pieces

1 medium onion, cut into wedges

8 tablespoons (1 stick) butter, melted

2 tablespoons all-purpose flour

COMBINE 1 1/2 gallons of cold water with the brine ingredients in a cooler large enough to hold the turkey, but small enough that you don't need too many additional gallons of brine to cover it. Brine the turkey for 24 hours. In cold weather, leave the cooler outdoors. Otherwise, place a gallon-size, sealable plastic bag filled with ice on top of the turkey and cover tightly. Add ice as necessary to keep the brine water cold.

REMOVE the turkey from the brine. Rinse and pat dry.

HEAT the oven to 325°F.

SPRINKLE the turkey cavity and skin with plenty of the dry rub. Sprinkle with the herbs to taste. Place the celery and onion in the cavity.

PLACE the bird in a turkey-size oven bag set in a roasting pan. Holding the bag open, brush the turkey with the butter.

Following the package directions for the oven bag, ADD the flour and cut the slits in the bag.

SEAL and bake for 15 minutes per pound, or until the internal temperature in the thigh is at least 175°F and the breast is 160°F.

LET the turkey rest for 10 to 15 minutes. Discard the onion and celery and carve.

Caveman Drums

We call R. B.'s house the Cave. His pals love his Shangri-la of music, motorcycles, guitars, cold beer, and firewood, where caveman chitchat comfortably drifts into menswear sales, paint colors, and advances in toaster oven technology.

Turkey drums fit the Cave scene with ease. All rubbed and sauced, Caveman Drums enable cavemen to maintain cavelike machismo while tiptoeing around the perimeter of their feelings. Bottled wing sauces are a cheater cinch, but, c'mon, be a man. Brush on a cheater interstate sauce (pages 38 to 43). You better have some stored in the fridge.

MAKES 6 SERVINGS

6 turkey drumsticks (about 4 pounds)

2 tablespoons oil

4 teaspoons Cheater Smoked Rub (page 47)

Barbecue sauce (optional)

HEAT the oven to 350°F.

MAKE two 3-drum foil packs for easy handling. For each pack, place three drumsticks on a sheet of heavy-duty aluminum foil large enough to seal tightly.

DRIZZLE 1 tablespoon of the oil over each pack of drumsticks, coating the skin until it's shiny. Sprinkle all sides of the drums with 2 teaspoons of the dry rub per foil pack.

SEAL the two packs and place them on a large rimmed baking sheet. Roast the turkey for 1½ hours, or until tender. Unwrap the packs and discard the juice.

HEAT the broiler. If saucing, brush the drumsticks with barbecue sauce before broiling. To crisp the skin, broil the drumsticks 4 inches from the heat source for about 5 minutes per side.

Five-Star Duck Legs

If you're a fan of dark-meat chicken, move up to Five-Star Duck Legs. The great thing is that it's getting much easier to find fresh duck breasts and legs, not just rock-hard frozen whole ducks that take a week to thaw. Pick one part, because breasts and legs are complete opposites. While the breasts are best cooked like a medium-rare steak, the legs are better slow-cooked like barbecue. Simple foil pouches make the whole procedure easy to manage. Duck legs reheat beautifully and take well to a brush-on glaze at the end.

MAKES 4 TO 6 SERVINGS

6 duck legs (about 3 pounds)

2 tablespoons Cheater Chinese Dry Rub (page 46)

For the glaze (optional)

1/4 cup honey

2 tablespoons soy sauce

HEAT the oven to 350°F.

SCORE or prick the duck legs with a knife to help release the fat during cooking.

MAKE two 3-leg foil packs for easy handling. For each pack, place three legs on a sheet of heavy-duty aluminum foil large enough to seal tightly around the legs. Sprinkle both sides of each leg with 1 teaspoon of the dry rub.

SEAL the packs and place them on a large rimmed baking sheet. Roast for 1½ to 2 hours, until the leg joint moves easily and the meat is tender.

OPEN the packs and pour off the excess fat. Serve the duck legs as is or finish them with the glaze under the broiler.

To make the glaze, if using, **COMBINE** the soy sauce and honey in a small bowl.

HEAT the broiler. Broil the legs about 4 inches from the heat source until crisp and browned, about 5 minutes. Brush the legs with the glaze and broil 2 to 3 minutes more.

CHAPTER 5

Cheater Beef and Lamb

Texas Beef Ribs

Despite his growing appreciation of cheater skills and methods, R. B. is still a little sore about the time his outdoor hickory smoked ribs (barely) lost the blind taste test against our cheater Texas Beef Ribs. Sorry, R. B., the kids preferred the smoky, supermoist, easy indoor version. The bigger surprise was finding a distinct outdoorlike crust on the slow cooker ribs. Because the ribs weren't simmering in sauce, the crust had a chance to develop. We didn't even need to finish them off under the broiler or on the grill.

In the pork-crazy mid-South, beef back ribs are a rarity. Now that the in-house tasting staff has ever-so-slightly favored the cheater style, we'll not hesitate to jump on a good-looking rack, regardless of the weather.

MAKES 4 TO 6 SERVINGS

4 pounds beef ribs

2 tablespoons Cheater Chili Dry Rub (page 45)

1/4 cup bottled smoke

CUT the ribs into 2-bone pieces and place them in a large slow cooker (at least 5 quarts).

SPRINKLE the dry rub on all sides of the ribs and add the bottled smoke.

COVER and cook on high for 4 to 6 hours or on low for 8 to 10 hours.

Hot Pot Beef Ribs

Put some big beefy ribs in a piping-hot cast-iron pot and in as little as an hour, the ribs will emerge with a deep, dark brown crust and a meaty, tender chew. Like slow cooker Texas Beef Ribs, there's no need to finish Hot Pot Ribs under a broiler unless you're brushing on a sauce. They also reheat well in a dry slow cooker or in a 350°F oven wrapped in foil.

You'll also get a nice batch of beef broth out of the deal. After it cools, chill the broth in the fridge to congeal the fat so you can discard it easily. Pour the warmed broth over the reheated ribs or freeze it to use in other recipes.

MAKES 4 TO 6 SERVINGS

5 pounds beef back ribs (2 racks of about 7 ribs each)

¼ cup cheater dry rub (you pick, pages 45 to 47)

HEAT the oven to 500°F. Place a large Dutch oven or enamel-coated cast-iron covered pot (at least 7 quarts) in the oven for 15 to 20 minutes.

With a sharp knife or a cleaver, CUT the racks into individual ribs. Rub the dry rub into all sides of the ribs.

Carefully LAY the ribs in the hot Dutch oven and cover. Immediately reduce the oven temperature to 300°F.

COOK the ribs for 45 minutes to 1 hour. The tender meat will shrink back from the end of the bone, but will stay connected to the bone for easy pickup.

Short Ribs of Beef

They're short, beefy, and full of flavor. Beef short ribs braised in rich red wine are a common restaurant staple, especially during cold weather. The meat turns out ultrasoft, rich, and stewy. Here short ribs are instead treated to the basic cheater slow cooker method without much added liquid. They turn out very tender, but still adhere to the bone. You can serve them on the bone or easily take the bones out for a pile of rich strands of meat. Use your dry rub choice to take the short ribs in different directions.

5 pounds beef short ribs

3 tablespoons cheater dry rub (you pick, pages 45 to 47)

4 garlic cloves, chopped

1/4 cup bottled smoke

PLACE the ribs in a large slow cooker (at least 5 quarts).

SPRINKLE with the dry rub and add the garlic and bottled smoke.

COVER and cook on high for 4 to 6 hours or on low for 8 to 10 hours.

Hobo Crock Chuck Flanken

Flanken-style ribs are beef short ribs cut across the bone (not parallel to the bone like short ribs), a half inch to an inch thick. This thin cut gives you a slice of beef with little oval rib bones evenly spaced throughout. Flanken-style ribs will turn mildly chewy and tender when slow-cooked long enough to render the fat and connective tissue. Since they like a little last-minute finish on a grill or under a broiler, they're a good choice for slow-cooking in advance. The high-heat finish brushed with Dijon mustard crusts up the meat juices. Brush the ribs with bottled smoke before slow cooking, if you like. Be sure to set the ground rules before dinner: Chewing on the rib bones is encouraged.

MAKES 6 SERVINGS

4 pounds chuck flanken-style ribs

2 tablespoons Cheater Basic Dry Rub (page 45)

Bottled smoke (optional)

About 1/2 cup Dijon mustard

PLACE the chuck flanken on a sheet of heavy-duty aluminum foil large enough to generously wrap around the meat.

RUB all sides of the ribs with the dry rub. Carefully lower the ribs, still on the foil, into a large slow cooker (at least 5 quarts). Brush with bottled smoke, if desired. Wrap the foil tightly around the ribs.

COVER and cook on high for 4 to 6 hours or on low for 8 to 10 hours.

Carefully LIFT the wrapped ribs out of the slow cooker and set on a rimmed baking sheet. Heat the broiler.

OPEN the foil and pour off any excess liquid. Brush all sides of the ribs liberally with the mustard.

BROIL the ribs about 4 inches from the heat source for 3 to 5 minutes per side, until browned and crusty. Be careful not to burn the mustard.

Korean Kalbi

Korean kalbi is soy-marinated chuck flanken-style beef ribs grilled quickly and eaten with rice wrapped in crisp lettuce leaves.

Our cheater kalbi uses the same soy-based marinade, but is cooked as a stew in the slow cooker. We usually swap the traditional flanken ribs for regular beef short ribs, which have larger bones that fall right out, leaving a nice pile of shredded meat. Short ribs are also easier for us to find.

Set the table taco-style with iceberg lettuce cups for shells. Along with the meat, stuff the lettuce shells with Korean kimchi, white rice, green onions, and hot peppers. We throw in some fresh cilantro, too.

MAKES 6 SERVINGS

For the kalbi

1½ cups soy sauce

¼ cup sugar

¼ cup toasted sesame oil

12 garlic cloves, chopped

1 heaping tablespoon chopped fresh ginger

6 green onions, sliced

4 to 5 pounds beef short ribs or chuck flanken-style ribs

Toasted sesame seeds (see page 67)

For serving

Iceberg lettuce cups, cooked white rice, kimchi, chopped jalapeño peppers, sliced green onions, and fresh cilantro sprigs

COMBINE the soy sauce, sugar, sesame oil, garlic, ginger, and green onions in a large slow cooker (at least 5 quarts). Stir until well blended.

ADD the ribs and blend well. Cover and cook on high for 4 to 6 hours or on low for 8 to 10 hours. The meat should be fall-apart tender.

SCOOP the meat out of the liquid and onto a platter and sprinkle with the sesame seeds.

SERVE the meat at the table with the lettuce cups, rice, and other accompaniments.

To serve the kalbi later, **REMOVE** the meat from the liquid and refrigerate. Pour the liquid into a separate container and refrigerate. After the liquid has chilled, remove the fat layer from the top and discard. Moisten the meat with some of the defatted juice and reheat in a saucepan over medium-low heat, in the slow cooker, or in a covered baking dish at 350°F for 20 to 30 minutes.

BASIC BRISKET

Beef brisket is a big, tough, flavorful cut of meat that needs foil, low heat, and plenty of time to be any good. It's not like a steak that you can cook over high heat to a nice rare pink. Without low, moist cooking for many uninterrupted hours, the connective tissue won't break down and tenderize the meat. The key is a 250°F oven to bring the brisket to a minimum internal temperature of 190°F or, even better, 200°F. It sounds too easy to screw up, but lots of rubber-tire brisket gets pushed out there, even from places claiming "real pit barbecue" status. Sorry, no sauce can save an undercooked or hot-cooked brisket.

In addition to a gentle method, you need a brisket with a good layer of fat (a fat cap). The fat is critical for tenderizing the meat as it cooks and for helping to absorb the smoke as well. Going lean won't save you anything. Just enjoy a good brisket and go for a walk instead.

Whole uncut briskets are 10 pounds or more. That means you'll usually find them already cut in half in the 4- to 6-pound range. Our best advice is to skip those very neat, trimmed little square briskets devoid of all fat. Cooking a brisket that small and lean won't be worth the time it takes. You're better off with a chuck roast.

Nicely sliced brisket on display at barbecue competitions is fine for the judges, but you can skip the showmanship at home. There's a fine line between tough, but easy-to-slice brisket, and fall-apart-tender brisket. For us, the best method is to cook the meat a day ahead so you can chill it before slicing against the grain. Cold brisket slices beautifully. Brisket reheats very nicely when warmed in its defatted beef juices in a 325°F oven for 20 to 30 minutes.

If your overnight brisket won't lift out of the foil without shredding apart, congratulations, and don't despair. Just get out your biggest cutting board and a sharp knife or cleaver, and carefully chop it up for chopped brisket. You won't lose points if it doesn't slice, not at the cheater competition, anyway.

Ultimate Cheater Brisket

Our friend Adele Franzblau doesn't see herself as a cook, but she cooks for her family every night and even has her own family cheater brisket recipe. She got it years ago for her son's bar mitzvah, when Adele's mother-in-law, Nancy, in Pampa, Texas, suggested Aunt Pat's Smoky Brisket.

Adele says she doesn't even measure. She sets the brisket on a big piece of foil and seasons it liberally with garlic salt, a half bottle of smoke, and about the same amount of Worcestershire sauce. The wrapped brisket marinates in the refrigerator overnight. The next morning, the brisket goes into a 250°F oven to cook unattended all day. When she gets home, the house smells wonderful, dinner's ready, and she's a hero.

Ultimate Cheater Brisket is similar, but with the added sweetness of a little onion and ketchup.

MAKES 8 TO 10 SERVINGS

1 medium onion, chopped

One 4- to 6-pound beef brisket

¼ cup Cheater Basic Dry Rub (page 45)

¼ cup ketchup

¼ cup Worcestershire sauce

¼ cup bottled smoke

SCATTER the onion in the center of a large sheet of heavy-duty aluminum foil. Rub all sides of the brisket with the dry rub and place the brisket on top of the onion.

COMBINE the ketchup, Worcestershire sauce, and bottled smoke in a small bowl and pour over the brisket.

Tightly WRAP the brisket in the foil and place in a roasting pan. Refrigerate for a few hours or overnight. When you're ready to cook, heat the oven to 250°F.

SLOW-ROAST the brisket for 6 to 8 hours. The meat should be fork-tender with an internal temperature of at least 190°F.

Hobo Crock 212 Brisket

*H*obo Crock 212 Brisket *combines outdoor cheater dry rub and indoor hobo crock cooking with traditional mother-in-law brisket ingredients. The slow cooker creates the moist low-heat environment critical for good brisket and, since it takes a while to cook, you can leave it for hours.*

Leftover brisket is extra good for any of the Two-Timing Cheater variations (see pages 176 to 187).

MAKES 6 TO 8 SERVINGS

One 3- to 4-pound beef brisket

2 to 3 tablespoons Cheater Basic Dry Rub (page 45)

One $14^{1}/_{2}$-ounce can diced tomatoes, drained

1 medium onion, chopped

3 garlic cloves, chopped

2 bay leaves

1 teaspoon dried oregano

PLACE the brisket on a sheet of heavy-duty aluminum foil large enough to generously wrap around the meat.

RUB all sides of the brisket with the dry rub. Carefully lower the brisket, still on the foil, into a large slow cooker (at least 5 quarts). Add the remaining ingredients and wrap the foil tightly around the brisket.

COVER and cook on high for 4 to 6 hours or on low for 8 to 10 hours. The meat should be fork-tender with an internal temperature of at least 190°F.

Carefully **LIFT** the wrapped brisket out of the slow cooker and set it on a rimmed baking sheet or large baking pan. Open the foil and allow the juices to collect in the pan. Move the brisket to a cutting board and thinly slice it against the grain. Serve with the warm meat juice.

Hobo Crock Chipotle Brisket

Chipotle peppers add deep, smoked heat to this cheater brisket, which is otherwise cooked with all the regular barbecue elements. The leftovers are outstanding, so cook the big one and stock up for your upcoming Mexican fiesta featuring brisket chili, nachos, tacos, or burritos.

....

MAKES 6 TO 8 SERVINGS

One 3- to 4-pound beef brisket

3 tablespoons Cheater Chili
   Dry Rub (page 45)

1 medium onion, chopped

4 or 5 garlic cloves, chopped

1/2 cup ketchup

1/4 cup Worcestershire sauce

1/4 cup cider vinegar

1/4 cup chopped chipotle
   peppers in adobo sauce

PLACE the brisket on a sheet of heavy-duty aluminum foil large enough to generously wrap around the meat. Rub all sides of the brisket with the dry rub.

Carefully LOWER the brisket, still on the foil, into a large slow cooker (at least 5 quarts). Sprinkle the onion and garlic over the meat.

COMBINE the ketchup, Worcestershire sauce, vinegar, and peppers in a small bowl. Pour the mixture over the brisket. Wrap the foil tightly around the meat.

COVER and cook on high for 4 to 6 hours or on low for 8 to 10 hours, until the internal temperature is at least 190°F and the meat is pull-apart tender.

Carefully LIFT the wrapped brisket out of the slow cooker and set it on a rimmed baking sheet or large baking pan. Open the foil and allow the juices to collect in the pan. Move the brisket to a cutting board and thinly slice it against the grain. Serve with the warm meat juice.

Low and Slow Texas Oven Brisket

For years R. B. could not stop falling for the latest food magazine pitch for perfectly smoked, tender beef brisket. Finally, after a twelve-hour ordeal of tending the fire and at least six episodes of wrapping and unwrapping and mopping, Min led him from the patio and into the kitchen and showed him around. Since that break-through, brisket is what's for dinner much more often.

Whether you're cooking indoors or out, the brisket's best friend is heavy-duty aluminum foil to trap moist heat and smoke. R. B.'s reformed oven method for brisket is to wrap it once, tuck it in a warm oven, and go to bed. Who needs melatonin with the aroma of a brisket wafting through the house in the wee hours? Be prepared to wake up ravenous.

MAKES 8 TO 10 SERVINGS

1 medium onion, chopped

6 garlic cloves, chopped

One 4- to 6-pound beef brisket with a layer of fat

3 to 4 tablespoons Cheater Chili Dry Rub (page 45)

1/4 cup bottled smoke

1/4 cup Worcestershire sauce

HEAT the oven to 250°F.

SCATTER the onion and garlic in the middle of a sheet of heavy-duty aluminum foil large enough to generously wrap around the meat. Lay the brisket on top and rub all sides with the dry rub. Pour the bottled smoke and Worcestershire over the meat.

SEAL the foil around the meat. Carefully place the foil pack in a large roasting pan. Roast the brisket for 7 to 9 hours, until the internal temperature is at least 190°F and the meat is pull-apart tender.

REMOVE the brisket from the oven. Open the foil and allow the juices to collect in the pan. Move the brisket to a cutting board and thinly slice it against the grain. Serve with the warm meat juices.

Hobo Chuck

There's nothing wrong with pot roast, but the beef chuck shoulder roast needs a break from the potatoes and carrots and soupy broth treatment. Beef chuck makes excellent barbecue, full of rich beefy flavor. Like brisket, its connective tissue requires slow barbecue-style cooking. Chuck isn't as long and stringy as brisket, but it can pretty much do anything a brisket can do and in less time. Also, a good chuck roast on special is an easier find than a brisket with a good fat cap. It's about choices and good substitutes, and a chuck roast is one of them.

MAKES 8 TO 10 SERVINGS

One 3- to 4-pound boneless chuck shoulder roast, trimmed of excess fat and cut into big chunks

3 tablespoons Cheater Basic Dry Rub (page 45)

¼ cup bottled smoke

PUT the roast in a medium to large slow cooker (at least 4 quarts).

SPREAD the dry rub over the meat. Add the bottled smoke.

COVER and cook on high for 4 to 6 hours or on low for 8 to 10 hours, until the meat shreds easily.

REMOVE the meat from the slow cooker and shred or chop.

Pulled Chuck Burgers

*T*he big idea here was to create hamburger-style meat in a slow cooker without the hassle of ground beef patties. We combined the flavors of a grilled burger, including the condiments, with the convenience of a slow-cooked chuck roast. The pickle juice really pulled it together.

After piling the meat on a bun with the usual backyard fixings, a member of our live-in focus group said, without any prompting whatsoever, "This tastes just like McDonald's!" We celebrated with dorky, teen-embarrassing high-fives all around.

A crock of pulled chuck burgers alongside a cooker filled with *Crock Dogs (page 71)* makes for the ultimate indoor hots and hams party. Consider this winning combo for kids' parties, tailgating, and a snowy or rainy or crowded Super Bowl. Look at this as another good reason for additional slow cookers. One just isn't enough, but you probably guessed that by now.

MAKES 10 TO 12 SERVINGS

One 3- to 4-pound boneless chuck roast, trimmed of excess fat and cut into 3-inch chunks

3 tablespoons Cheater Basic Dry Rub (page 45)

1/2 cup ketchup

1/2 cup pickle juice from hamburger dill chips

1/4 cup bottled smoke

1/4 cup yellow mustard

6 garlic cloves, chopped

For the hamburger fixings

Hamburger buns, mustard, ketchup, hamburger dill chips, sliced cheese, lettuce, and onion and tomato slices

PLACE the meat in a medium to large slow cooker (at least 4 quarts) and coat evenly with the dry rub. Add the ketchup, pickle juice, bottled smoke, mustard, and garlic and blend well.

COVER and cook on high for 4 to 6 hours or on low for 8 to 10 hours, until the meat shreds easily.

SERVE the pulled chuck mounded on buns with hamburger fixings.

One-Hour Rump or Round Roast

*T*he rump roast and the eye of round roast are two ornery beef cuts from the cow's rear. They pack great beef flavor, but overcooked they are an embarrassingly tough chew. We prefer quick high-heat roasting to slow cooking so that the meat is just medium rare. Cut paper-thin, it makes excellent roast beef sandwiches. A mustard and dry rub paste turns good and crusty during the high-heat cooking. Allow the meat to sit tented under foil a good twenty minutes before you attempt any carving. An electric knife is ideal for thin slices that beg for a crisp sandwich roll.

One 4-pound rump or eye of round roast

¼ cup cheater dry rub (you pick, pages 45 to 47)

3 tablespoons Dijon mustard

2 tablespoons bottled smoke

HEAT the oven to 500°F. Place the roast on a rack in a medium roasting pan.

BLEND the dry rub and mustard into a paste in a small bowl. Spread the paste on all sides of the roast with your fingers. Sprinkle the smoke over the roast.

ROAST for 15 minutes. Reduce the heat to 300°F and roast 45 minutes more for rare. The internal temperature should be 115°F.

REMOVE the roast from the oven, cover loosely with foil, and let rest at least 20 minutes before slicing. Serve thinly sliced.

Cheater Kitchen Burgers

This indoor burger recipe make six burgers (too many for one pan), so use the broiler or finish the pan-seared burgers all at once in the oven. Ground beef is available in plenty of designer styles and fat-to-lean ratios. Use what you like. Remember that the higher fat content varieties like chuck have a rich, juicy taste and a smoother texture than the leaner ones, which tend to be dry and grainy. Chuck will also spatter up your stovetop and broiler a bit more. Either way, good ventilation is important.

Burger doneness is an individual right that the government recommends you exercise at 160°F for proper food safety. Whatever temperature you pick, remove the burgers from heat when they are about 5 degrees below that target as the temperature will continue to rise while the meat rests. R. B. himself goes into fits above 130°F. He's still with us, knock on wood, despite rare burgers and the raw oysters he downs with abandon.

MAKES 6 BURGERS

2 pounds ground chuck or other ground beef

1 tablespoon Worcestershire sauce

1 tablespoon Cheater Basic Dry Rub (page 45)

1 tablespoon bottled smoke

For Broiler Burgers

HEAT the broiler. Place a large rimmed baking sheet in the oven to heat.

COMBINE the meat, Worcestershire sauce, dry rub, and bottled smoke in a large bowl and mix well.

DIVIDE the meat into 6 equal portions. Form patties about 1 inch thick (or whatever size you like). Carefully place the patties on the hot baking sheet.

BROIL the burgers to your liking, 8 to 10 minutes. Flip them only if you feel like it.

For Skillet-Seared Oven Burgers

HEAT the oven to 450°F.

(continued)

COMBINE the meat, Worcestershire sauce, dry rub, and bottled smoke in a large bowl and mix well.

DIVIDE the meat into 6 equal portions. Form patties about 1 inch thick.

BROWN the burgers, three at a time, in a very hot skillet (cast iron works best) over high heat, about 2 minutes per side. Transfer all the burgers to a large rimmed baking sheet.

FINISH the burgers in the oven until cooked to your liking. Check the internal temperature after 5 minutes.

Kitchen Burg-anza!

It's just a theory, but Min believes that men today are better cooks and super-market shoppers because of warehouse and mega hardware stores. The behavioral phenomenon of pushing a grocery cart has built up the male tolerance and stamina for critical shopping skills—browsing, locating, discriminating, and deciding from among the hundreds of options on any store aisle.

Our burgers are tailor-made for all the guys out there who shop and cook and have evolved beyond frozen patties, pickle chips, and yellow mustard.

Besto Pesto Burger

These are an excellent choice for late summer when fresh tomatoes are at their besto.

6 thick, juicy Cheater Kitchen Burgers (page 119)

For the Besto Pesto Sauce
1/2 cup mayonnaise
1/4 cup prepared pesto
2 tablespoons Dijon mustard

For serving
6 slices Italian bread, toasted
6 slices fresh mozzarella cheese
6 slices ripe tomato
Fresh basil leaves (optional)

COOK the burgers.

COMBINE the mayonnaise, pesto, and mustard in a small bowl.

PLACE the warm burgers on the toasted bread.

SPREAD each burger with the Besto Pesto Sauce and top with a slice of cheese and tomato. Dollop each with additional sauce and garnish with a basil leaf, if you want.

CHEATER BEEF AND LAMB

······································

Burgos de Mayo

Cinco de Mayo actually marks the 1862 Mexican victory over the French, not Mexican Independence Day, as some believe. Thanks to Madison Avenue, it's a holiday more enthusiastically embraced north of the border than south. To celebrate this semicorporate affair, grilled Burgos de Mayo combine all our favorite Mexican flavors (including the tequila) on one bun. Top them off with Mayo de Mayo, our Cinco "special sauce."

For the burgers
1 1/2 pounds ground chuck
1/2 pound chorizo, cooked and crumbled
2 tablespoons tequila
1 tablespoon fresh lime juice
1/2 teaspoon garlic salt
6 slices pepper Jack cheese

For the Mayo de Mayo
3 tablespoons mayonnaise
3 tablespoons salsa
3 tablespoons chopped fresh cilantro
3 tablespoons sliced green onions
1 1/2 teaspoons chili powder

For serving
6 large hamburger buns, toasted
Iceberg lettuce leaves

COMBINE the meats, tequila, lime juice, and garlic salt in a mixing bowl. Form the meat into 6 patties.

COOK as directed for Cheater Kitchen Burgers (see page 119). During the last minute or two of cooking, top with cheese.

COMBINE all the sauce ingredients in a small bowl.

PLACE the burgers on the buns and serve with Mayo de Mayo and lettuce.

....

The Daddy Melt

Our other favorite Nashville chicken joint, McDougal's Village Coop, is renowned for its fried chicken tenders, Peyton Manning's UT Knoxville fridge door bolted to the ceiling, and kegs of local Yazoo beer on tap. We renamed our favorite patty melt the "Daddy Melt" after owner Tommy McDougal announced the news of his first child and because it was his late stepdad Tanksley Foster's favorite lunch. Unfortunately, the burger's success led to its extinction. It was just too popular for a place whose motto is "Chicken and Beer."

2 medium Cheater Fajita Onions (page 172)
6 thick, juicy Cheater Kitchen Burgers (page 119)
6 slices American cheese
12 slices thick white bread

PREPARE the Cheater Fajita Onions and set aside. The onions can be made ahead.

COOK the burgers. Top with cheese during the last minute or two of cooking. Meanwhile, toast the bread and warm the onions.

PLACE a burger on a piece of toast. Top generously with onions and cover with toast. Serve hot.

CHEATER BEEF AND LAMB

The Dip's Guac Burger

Back when our friend Claire Mullally owned Bobbie's Dairy Dip, a '50s-style ice cream and burger drive-in, she organized Sunday night parking lot jam sessions to drum up a little business in the cooler fall months. Where else but Nashville can you see Country Music Award and Grammy Award winners and nominees play for tips with no cover charge and a side of sweet potato fries? The jam band was complete when a cab arrived straight from the airport carrying Claire's husband, songwriter/musician Greg Trooper, just landing from a tour with John Prine.

The standing room only parking lot was rocking with loyal Dip families filling up on live music, behemoth burgers, and soft-serve sundaes. The only thing missing was a beer truck. Claire juggled the kitchen, the counter, and managed to sing back-up on a cranking cover of "Love the One You're With."

Our version of the Dip's guac burger is a beauty featuring a juicy beef patty adorned with cheese, a smear of guacamole, salsa, sour cream, tomato and onion, and jalapeño slices instead of pickles.

MAKES 6 SERVINGS

6 Cheater Kitchen Burgers (page 119)

2 ripe medium Hass avocados

Garlic salt

Juice of ½ lemon

6 large hamburger buns, toasted

For serving

Salsa, sour cream, and sliced pickled jalapeños to taste

Lettuce leaves and fresh tomato and red onion slices

6 slices cheddar cheese

COOK the burgers. Top each with a slice of cheese.

MASH the avocado flesh with garlic salt to taste and lemon juice until smooth with a few chunks in a small bowl.

PLACE the cheeseburgers on the buns. Top with a generous dollop of guacamole, salsa, and sour cream. Add jalapeño, lettuce, tomato, and onion.

Fridge Door Special Sauce Burger

Stephen Cellar, R. B.'s hungry nephew, asked R. B. where he got that awesome red sauce we had served with burgers at a family picnic. Having grown up in the sophisticated chipotle-buffalo-ranch-bruschetta drive-through era, Stephen didn't recognize that good old twentieth-century American favorite, "special sauce."

When we grew up, McDonald's special sauce on a Big Mac was the first condiment other than mustard, ketchup, and mayonnaise that anyone considered for a burger. Way before pesto, sun-dried tomatoes, and made-up foreign-sounding food names, even the pedestrian "special sauce" was fancy enough to attract attention. How long did it take us to figure out that it was just like Thousand Island dressing?

The mystery ingredient was chili sauce, that misnamed cousin to ketchup shelved beside the cocktail sauces. It looks and tastes like ketchup, but not quite as sweet or silky smooth and without any apparent chili flavor.

For a fancy presentation, serve bunless chopped-steak burgers alongside crisp iceberg wedges and ripe tomato slices adorned with thinly sliced red onion, crumbled bacon, and Fridge Door Special Sauce. Or, slather over burgers topped with lettuce, cheese, pickles, and onions on a sesame seed bun. It's so old, it's new again.

MAKES 6 SERVINGS

For the Fridge Door Special Sauce

1/2 cup mayonnaise

1/4 cup chili sauce (or substitute ketchup)

1/4 cup sweet pickle relish (sometimes we use chopped hamburger dills)

Dash of Worcestershire sauce

Dash of hot pepper sauce

6 Cheater Kitchen Burgers (page 119)

6 large hamburger buns, toasted

COMBINE the mayonnaise, chili sauce, relish, Worcestershire sauce, and hot pepper sauce in a small bowl. Blend well.

COOK the burgers.

PLACE the burgers on the buns. Slather on the sauce and pile on other toppings of your choice.

Broiler Steaks with Chimichurri

We had never considered grilling monster kebabs of unidentifiable cuts of meat until we spotted those churrascaria ads in airline magazines. The Brazilian barbecue called churrasco (pronounced shoo-RAS-koo) prepared on oversized spits looks especially good when you're strapped in a seat at 35,000 feet with only a tiny bag of peanuts.

At home, a family-size sirloin, some rib eyes, or beef tenderloin steaks taste just as Brazilian with a side of chimichurri, the traditional spicy mix of fresh cilantro and parsley, onions, garlic, vinegar, and olive oil. We oil up and simply season the steaks with nothing more than salt and pepper before searing under a hot broiler. Instead of bothering with cutting the meat into chunks for skewers, cook the steaks whole and carve them into thick slices before serving. Everyone at the table can see the doneness of the pieces and can choose how much and what they want.

Complete the meal with Cuban Black Beans (page 149), rice, and some kind of salad with hearts of palm thrown in. R. B. recommends a spoonful or two of chimichurri in scrambled eggs with cold steak for brunch.

COMBINE all the chimichurri ingredients in a food processor and pulse until finely chopped. Spoon into a small bowl, cover, and refrigerate until serving time.

MAKES 4 TO 6 SERVINGS

For the chimichurri

1 medium bunch fresh cilantro, washed and dried, thick stems removed

1 medium bunch fresh parsley, washed and dried, thick stems removed

1 garlic clove, minced

1 small sweet onion

1/4 cup red wine vinegar

1/3 cup olive oil

Kosher salt and black pepper to taste

Red pepper flakes to taste

For the steak

3 pounds boneless sirloin, rib eye, or beef tenderloin, cut into steaks 1 to 1 1/2 inches thick

Olive oil

Kosher salt and black pepper

HEAT the broiler. Coat the steaks liberally with olive oil and sprinkle with salt and pepper.

BROIL about 4 inches from the heat source for 7 minutes on the first side. Flip the steaks and broil for 3 to 6 minutes on the second side, until the internal temperature reaches 120°F for medium rare.

LET the steaks rest for 10 minutes before carving into 1-inch slices. Serve the slices on a platter with the chimichurri on the side.

House Lamb Shanks

Lamb shanks cooked in the cheater slow cooker without a lot of the usual braising liquid turn out with an amazing chestnut brown patina. We swear they look more like they came off an open fire of crackling grapevines than out of Min's limited-edition NASCAR Bobby Labonte slow cooker. In a few hours and with very little liquid, the meat cooks to a perfectly tender state, but stays beautifully intact for country-chic presentation.

Imagine the shanks piled on a deep platter with garlicky white beans and wilted escarole or on fashionable couscous. Talk about restaurant-stylish and dinner-party perfect.

Unlike last-minute chops, shanks taste best made ahead and reheated. Depending on your final destination, reheat them in the slow cooker by themselves or foil wrapped in the oven with side dishes. Shanks are also an efficient way to achieve a pile of tender pulled lamb for pita pockets piled with Yo Mayo Slaw (page 152) or paired with the Detailed Salad (page 156). We like to use the Rub de la Maison, which combines barbecue basics with herbes de Provence and dried lemon peel.

MAKES 6 TO 8 SERVINGS

6 lamb shanks (about 5 pounds)

3 tablespoons Cheater Rub de la Maison (page 47)

1/4 cup bottled smoke

PLACE the shanks in a large slow cooker (at least 5 quarts) and sprinkle the meat with the dry rub. Add the bottled smoke.

COVER and cook on high for 4 to 6 hours or on low for 8 to 10 hours. The meat should be fork-tender.

Cheater Q'Balls

We've always had a thing for the charred lamb kebabs on flat skewers that the kebab/gyro joints do so well. One place even gave R. B. a couple of swordlike skewers after he bombarded them with questions. We make lamb/beef combo meatballs flavored with cumin to roast in the oven, and sometimes even finish on the grill. The meatballs cook on a baking sheet just like a pan of cookies.

We've come to appreciate the many lives of a good batch of meatballs. A bag of Q'Balls in the freezer is as prized as a bag of brisket. Toss them with pasta, stuff them into pita pockets and sub sandwiches, serve them as a heavy appetizer or a quick heat-up for kid suppers. Customize the Q'Balls by substituting a couple teaspoons of any of the cheater dry rubs for the salt and seasonings.

MAKES 8 SERVINGS (ABOUT 36 MEATBALLS)

1/2 cup bread crumbs

2 tablespoons bottled smoke plus enough water to equal 1/2 cup

2 large eggs

1 pound ground beef

1 pound ground lamb

4 garlic cloves, minced

1/4 cup chopped fresh parsley

2 teaspoons cumin or 2 teaspoons dried oregano

1 teaspoon kosher salt

1/2 teaspoon black pepper

HEAT the oven to 375°F.

COMBINE the bread crumbs and the smoky water in a large bowl. Stir in the eggs.

ADD the remaining ingredients and blend well without overworking.

FORM golf-ball-size meatballs and place on a large rimmed baking sheet.

BAKE for 30 to 35 minutes, until the internal temperature reaches 160°F.

CHAPTER 6

Cheater Seafood

Ultimate Cheater
Oven-Smoked Salmon

For oven salmon we use either an enamel-coated roasting pan or a foil-lined baking sheet. As much as we love cast iron for its searing qualities and overall old-school cooking coolness, fishy bacon and cornbread are never a big hit with the breakfast club. Any salmon leftovers are earmarked for Two-Timer Salmon Salad (recipe follows).

It helps to cut whole salmon fillets into serving-size pieces before cooking. Pay attention to the thickness of the fish (the very thin ends take almost no time) and cook accordingly.

MAKES 4 SERVINGS

2 tablespoons vegetable oil

Four 6-ounce salmon fillets, rinsed and patted dry

1 tablespoon bottled smoke

4 teaspoons Basic Cheater Dry Rub (page 45)

1 lemon, zested and cut into wedges

HEAT the oven to 500°F. Pour the oil onto a roasting pan or rimmed baking sheet. Place the pan in the oven and wait for the oil to begin smoking.

While the pan heats up, BRUSH the salmon with the bottled smoke. Sprinkle each piece liberally with the dry rub and the lemon zest.

Carefully PLACE the fillets in the hot pan. If they have skin, place them skin side up. Cook for 3 minutes. Flip the salmon and cook for an additional 2 minutes. Cooking time depends on the thickness of the fillets. The internal temperature of the fish should be about 125°F and the inside should look slightly translucent. The fish will continue to cook once out of the oven.

SERVE warm with lemon wedges or chill it for serving the next day.

··

Two-Timer Salmon Salad

$1/2$ **pound chilled Ultimate Cheater Oven-Smoked Salmon (about 2 cups), flaked**

2 celery ribs, chopped

$1/3$ **cup mayonnaise**

1 tablespoon Dijon mustard

Fresh lemon juice to taste

1 hard-cooked egg, chopped (optional)

COMBINE all the ingredients in a bowl. Serve chilled.

Fridge Lox

One of the cool things about cooking cheater barbecue is the thought that something is going on inside that slow cooker or behind the oven door while you're off doing something else. The same is true with making lox in the fridge.

MAKES 4 SERVINGS

1/4 cup brown sugar

1/4 cup kosher salt

1 tablespoon bottled smoke

1 pound very fresh salmon fillet with or without skin, rinsed and patted dry

1 bunch fresh dill (optional)

Our method is just a simple take on classic cold smoking with a little bottled smoke. The fish "cooks" in sugar and salt and cold-smokes in the fridge. Three days later, like magic, you're in lox. Serve with toasted bagels and cream cheese or dark rye bread with chopped hard-cooked egg, capers, and red onion.

COMBINE the sugar, salt, and bottled smoke in a small bowl and blend into a paste.

LAY the salmon (skin side down) on a piece of plastic wrap large enough to completely seal the fish. Spread the paste over the fish. Top with the dill, if using.

SEAL the fish tightly in the plastic wrap and set it in a dish that will catch the juices.

PLACE a clean, foil-wrapped brick on top of the fish and refrigerate. The lox will be smoked and cured in three days.

UNWRAP the fish and discard the dill. Transfer the fish to a board and thinly slice on the diagonal with a sharp knife.

Tied-Up Trout

Trout is a popular fish in a landlocked state like Tennessee. It's fresh, easy, and quick to cook on a grill or in the oven. The presentation of a whole fish at home conjures up the rustic feel of a riverbank campout, and the burnt string used to lash together the lemon-and-dill-stuffed fish creates a real dinner-under-the-stars mood. Complete the faux angler's mess with Oven Potatoes (page 167) and a green salad with your own smoked paprika vinaigrette.

MAKES 4 SERVINGS

4 whole rainbow trout, dressed (about 1 pound each)

Olive oil

Kosher salt and black pepper

3 lemons, thinly sliced, plus 1 lemon, cut into wedges

Fresh dill sprigs

Bottled smoke

HEAT the oven to 500°F.

RINSE the trout and pat dry, inside and out. Rub the cavity and skin with olive oil and sprinkle with salt and pepper to taste.

LAY 3 or 4 lemon slices and a few dill sprigs in each fish cavity. To secure the lemon and dill, tie each fish three times, once in the middle and once at each end.

PLACE the fish on a baking sheet and brush lightly with bottled smoke and olive oil.

ROAST the fish for 10 to 15 minutes. To check for doneness, cut through the skin and into the meat on one fish. The white flesh should flake easily.

CUT and remove the strings. Serve one fish per person with lemon wedges. The backbone is easy to lift out with a fork as you work through the fillets.

Safety First Oyster Roast

Fresh briny oysters out of a jar satisfy our periodic oyster craving without the hassle of shucking. To cheat, swap the half shell for a casserole dish and dress the oysters with smoky shallots, butter, and lemon. A few minutes under the broiler and you've got a seaside party anywhere, anytime. Slurp them up with saltines. Cold beer, sparkling wine, and dry white wine are what we're drinking.

....

MAKES 4 SERVINGS

1 pound fresh oysters (about 24), drained (buy the jarred ones like we do or have your fishmonger shuck them for you)

4 tablespoons ($^1/_2$ stick) butter

2 medium shallots, finely chopped (about $^1/_4$ cup)

$^1/_4$ cup dry white wine

2 tablespoons fresh lemon juice

2 teaspoons bottled smoke

Kosher salt

Freshly cracked black pepper

Chopped fresh parsley

For serving

Saltines, hot pepper sauce, and lemon wedges

PLACE the oysters in a pie plate or gratin dish in a single layer.

MELT the butter in a small skillet. Cook the shallots in the butter over medium heat until softened, about 5 minutes.

STIR in the wine, lemon juice, and bottled smoke. Season with a pinch of salt.

COOK an additional 3 minutes to reduce the sauce until slightly thickened. Meanwhile, heat the broiler.

POUR the sauce over the oysters and season with pepper. Broil the oysters about 4 inches from the heat source for 5 minutes.

SPRINKLE with parsley. Serve with saltines, hot pepper sauce, and lemon wedges.

Rhode Island Clambake in a Bowl

*T*his stovetop stew is a loose interpretation of the three-day beachside fest known as the New England clambake, that picture-perfect steaming seaweed pit immortalized each August by every shiny food magazine. How do all those beautiful people stay so crisp and clean after digging a sand pit and hauling rocks? One summer, on the beach in Charlestown, Rhode Island, we were actually asked by the crew of a popular food television program to stay out of camera range until they finished a shoot. Our cluttered site didn't convey casual flawlessness.

Rhode Island Clambake in a Bowl is not only less work, it's a much cheaper cheater because we're skipping the lobster. Instead of a plate of steamed seafood with a little piece of corn on the cob, a sausage link, and a stray potato, this stew is meant to be served in bowls, with bread for sopping up the clam broth.

MELT the butter in a large Dutch oven or heavy soup pot with a lid. Add the onion and cook over medium heat until softened, 5 to 7 minutes.

While the onion cooks, **BROWN** the sausage in a large skillet.

ADD the sausage, potatoes, wine, and water to the onion. Bring the broth to a boil over high heat. Reduce the heat and simmer, partially covered, until the potatoes are just tender, 20 to 30 minutes.

....

MAKES 6 SERVINGS

4 tablespoons ($\frac{1}{2}$ stick) butter

1 medium onion, chopped

1 pound smoked sausage, mild or spicy, quartered and cut into small chunks

3 medium red potatoes, cut into $\frac{1}{2}$-inch cubes (3 to 4 cups)

2 cups dry white wine

2 cups water or 1 cup clam juice and 1 cup water

One 16-ounce package frozen corn, thawed

Kosher salt

4 dozen cherrystone clams, rinsed and soaked in ice water

Chopped fresh parsley

For serving

Lemon slices, hot pepper sauce, and warm French bread

STIR in the corn and bring to a boil. Season the broth lightly with salt to taste. Reduce the heat, add the clams, and cover the pot. Simmer until the clams open, 5 to 7 minutes. Discard any clams that don't open. Spoon the stew into large bowls and top with parsley. Serve with lemon slices, hot pepper sauce, and bread.

Catfish Sticks

Next to firing up the smoker, having a catfish fry in the party pot (our name for the turkey fryer) is our preferred all-day patio workout. Then, after hours of fun over the hot cauldron, we're done with frying for months. Except maybe for an occasional batch of corn tortilla chips.

The thing about catfish is that its soft, almost mushy flesh demands a rigid cornmeal exoskeleton forged in hot peanut oil. An oven and a seasoned panko/cornmeal crust mimic the deep-fried crust with a fraction of the mess and without oil recycling in the morning.

R. B. confirms that leftover Catfish Sticks reheat like a dream in a toaster oven. He makes a mean cheater po'boy with reheated catfish sticks piled on a hamburger bun slathered with tartar sauce and topped with iceberg lettuce excavated from the crisper drawer.

MAKES 4 TO 6 SERVINGS (ABOUT 32 FISH STICKS)

4 catfish fillets (about 2 pounds), rinsed and patted dry

¼ cup peanut oil or vegetable oil

1 cup panko bread crumbs

2 tablespoons cornmeal

4 teaspoons Cheater Basic Dry Rub (page 45)

HEAT the oven to 450°F. Lightly coat a large rimmed baking sheet with nonstick cooking spray.

CUT the fillets into quarters lengthwise. Cut each of the four strips in half, making 8 fingers per fillet.

PLACE the catfish fingers and the oil in a large bowl and toss to coat evenly.

PLACE the panko, cornmeal, and dry rub in a shallow bowl and blend well. Roll each catfish finger in the breading and place it on the baking sheet.

BAKE for 10 to 15 minutes, until the fish is crispy outside and tender inside. The thicker pieces will need a minute or two longer to cook. If a finger seems tough when pierced with the tip of a knife, cook it a little longer.

Panko Parmesan
Rub-Crusted Scallops

*O*nce *you start using the lighter, larger, crisper Japanese panko crumbs, the usual bread crumbs will feel like sand. A box of panko in the pantry crunches up all kinds of oven-fried seafood and chicken and substitutes for bread crumbs in any recipe. Their airy texture is akin to the difference between flaky kosher salt and dense iodized salt. Figure on about three large scallops per person.*

MAKES 6 SERVINGS

2$\frac{1}{2}$ pounds large sea scallops (about 18)

8 tablespoons (1 stick) butter, melted

$\frac{3}{4}$ cup panko bread crumbs

$\frac{1}{4}$ cup grated Parmesan cheese

1 tablespoon Cheater Basic Dry Rub (page 45)

Chopped fresh parsley

1 lemon, zested and cut into wedges

HEAT the oven to 450°F. Lightly coat a large rimmed baking sheet with nonstick cooking spray.

RINSE the scallops and pat dry. Place the scallops in a large bowl with 6 tablespoons of the melted butter. Gently toss to coat evenly.

COMBINE the panko, Parmesan, and dry rub in a shallow bowl and blend well.

ROLL each scallop in the breading and place on the baking sheet.

BAKE the scallops for 10 minutes. Remove them from the oven and heat the broiler.

SPRINKLE the tops lightly with any leftover breading and drizzle with the remaining 2 tablespoons of butter.

BROIL the scallops about 4 inches from the heat source for 3 to 5 minutes, until the tops are golden brown and crisp.

SPRINKLE with parsley and lemon zest and serve with the lemon wedges.

Smoky Shrimp and Sausage Boil

A traditional low-country boil is a whole lot easier in a kitchen than on a deck with all that huge pot, outdoor burner, and propane tank business. Usually, the corn on the cob and the new potatoes are cooked right in the boil with everything else, but in a regular kitchen stockpot, we think it's easier to cook the vegetables separately. We like the extra depth that a little bottled smoke adds to the shrimp boil.

MAKES 6 SERVINGS

1 beer (12 ounces)

1/2 cup Old Bay seasoning

2 tablespoons kosher salt

1/4 cup bottled smoke

2 to 3 celery ribs with leaves, cut into 2- to 3-inch pieces

2 lemons, quartered

1 pound fully cooked smoked sausage (mild or hot), cut into 1/2-inch pieces

2 pounds large shrimp (16 to 20 count), peeled and deveined

Boiled new potatoes and corn on the cob

COMBINE a gallon of water, the beer, Old Bay, salt, bottled smoke, and celery in a large stockpot. Squeeze the lemon quarters over the broth and add the pieces to the pot.

BRING the broth to a boil. Add the sausage and reduce the heat to keep the pot at a steady low boil. Simmer about 5 minutes.

INCREASE the heat to return the liquid to a rolling boil. Add the shrimp and cook until pink and opaque throughout, 4 to 5 minutes.

DRAIN the shrimp and sausage into a colander and discard the broth.

SERVE the shrimp and sausage in a large bowl with boiled new potatoes and corn on the cob.

Smoky Boiled and Pickled Shrimp

Pickled shrimp remind us of the time when R. B. was on his home brew jag. As usual, he was way ahead of his time. Now a slightly smarter man, R. B. relies instead on the craftsmanship of real brew artisans for his lagers, ales, stouts, and porters.

Back to these delicious shrimp and why we're distracted by beer. Pickled shrimp must relax in the refrigerator a while to soak up the flavors of the oniony marinade. As with beer fermentation and the curing of Fridge Lox (page 134), you must leave them alone and go find something else to do. Meanwhile, things are happening. Easier than making beer, pickling shrimp takes an overnight instead of three weeks. Min occasionally tosses in a chopped fresh green jalapeño (with the seeds). We cannot get enough of these.

For the boil, **COMBINE** a gallon of water, the beer, Old Bay, salt, and bottled smoke. Bring to a rolling boil.

ADD the shrimp and cook for 4 to 5 minutes, until pink and opaque throughout.

DRAIN the shrimp in a colander and discard the boil. You can leave the tails on or take them off.

For pickling, **PLACE** the shrimp in a large bowl and toss with the onion.

COMBINE the remaining pickling ingredients in a small bowl and whisk with a fork. Pour the marinade over the shrimp and toss to coat evenly.

COVER and refrigerate; serve within a day or two.

MAKES 6 SERVINGS

For the smoky boil

1 beer (12 ounces)

1/2 cup Old Bay seasoning

2 tablespoons kosher salt

1/4 cup bottled smoke

2 pounds large shrimp (16 to 20 count), peeled and deveined

For the pickling marinade

1 medium onion, cut into thin slivers

1/2 cup olive oil

1/2 cup red wine vinegar

1 tablespoon celery seed

1 tablespoon mustard seeds

4 bay leaves, crushed

Black pepper to taste

BBQ Garlic Shrimp

New Orleans–style barbecued shrimp, called "barbecue" even though they have nothing to do with smoke or a grill, are usually prepared in the oven. We do ours in a big hot pot on the stove because this dish is all about the buttery, garlicky sauce. Mass quantities of crusty French bread are required for sopping.

We plunk the big pot in the middle of the table and go to town. It's an exceptionally good time tearing into long baguettes and washing everything down with plenty of cold white wine. Sometimes, we remember the salad.

MAKES 6 SERVINGS

¼ cup bottled smoke

¼ cup kosher salt

2 pounds large shrimp (16 to 20 count), peeled and deveined

For the BBQ Garlic Sauce

8 tablespoons (1 stick) butter, melted

¼ cup olive oil

¼ cup fresh lemon juice

2 tablespoons Worcestershire sauce

2 tablespoons hot pepper sauce

6 garlic cloves, minced

Black pepper to taste

COMBINE 1 quart of cold water, the bottled smoke, and salt in a large bowl. Stir to dissolve the salt.

ADD the shrimp to the bowl, cover, and chill for about 30 minutes. Drain, pat the shrimp dry, and discard the brine.

While brining the shrimp, **COMBINE** all the ingredients for the BBQ Garlic Sauce in a small bowl.

TOSS the sauce with the brined shrimp. To make ahead, cover and refrigerate, then cook the shrimp just before serving.

To cook the shrimp, **HEAT** a large cast-iron skillet or enamel-coated cast-iron pot over high heat until piping hot. Carefully place the shrimp in the pot and cook, stirring frequently, until pink and opaque throughout, 3 to 5 minutes depending upon the size of the shrimp. Avoid overcooking the shrimp because they will turn rubbery in a hurry.

Dry-Rubbed Oven Shrimp Skewers

Whenever the two-pound bags of frozen shrimp are on sale (the bigger the shrimp, the better), we throw one in the freezer and the other in a brine before a quick trip under the broiler. If you're not near live shrimp, choose bagged frozen ones because the fish counter's fresh is often the same stuff already thawed. You'll get perkier results thawing them in a salty bath, which puts a little ocean back in.

This recipe is ripe for tinkering. Vary the rub and swap the butter for olive oil. If you skip the brine, use a dry rub with salt instead. Smoked sea salts and smoked paprika chic it up, but the bare-bones version is always a home run with kids. Pull a skewer through a warm corn or flour tortilla, and top with shredded cabbage, cilantro, onion, and a quick chili powder mayonnaise, à la fish tacos. Delicious.

MAKES 6 SERVINGS

1/4 cup bottled smoke

1/4 cup kosher salt

2 pounds large shrimp (16 to 20 count), peeled and deveined

2 tablespoons Cheater No-Salt Dry Rub (page 47)

4 tablespoons (1/2 stick) butter, melted

COMBINE 1 quart of cold water, the bottled smoke, and salt in a large bowl. Stir to dissolve the salt.

ADD the shrimp to the bowl, cover, and chill for about 30 minutes. Drain, pat the shrimp dry, and discard the brine.

While brining the shrimp, SOAK ten to twelve 8- or 10-inch bamboo skewers in water for at least 30 minutes.

HEAT the oven to 500°F.

TOSS the brined shrimp with the dry rub in a medium bowl until well coated. Thread 4 or 5 shrimp per skewer so that the shrimp are not touching each other. Lay the skewers on a baking sheet. Brush the shrimp with the melted butter.

BAKE for about 5 minutes, or until the shrimp are pink and opaque throughout.

CHAPTER 7

Cheater Sides

Boston Crocked Beans

Pecos Pintos

Tennessee White Beans

Cuban Black Beans

Burnt Ends Beans

Cheater BBQ Slaw

Yo Mayo Slaw

Q-Cumbers

Cheater Sweet Pickles and Peños

Sweet Corn in the Cup

Detailed Salad with Three Creamy Dressings

Oven-Charred-Pineapple Salads

Cranberry Fruit Salad

Broiled Corn and Rice Salad

Potato Salad

Hot-Oven Cauliflower

Oven Packet Vegetables

Get Along Roasted Roots

Micro-Broiled Winter Squash

Cheater Fajita Onions

Asian Greens

Boston Crocked Beans

It's no big deal to make a pot of real "baked" beans, especially if you forget about the baking part and use a slow cooker. The only work is cooking the bacon and onion before dumping everything into the crock.

Boston beans have lots in common with barbecue. The vital ingredients—molasses, mustard, onion, and bacon—are the same components that impart the barbecue balance of sweet/sour/savory in sauces. In the slow cooker, the beans finish up just as thick and dark as any from Boston.

MAKES 8 TO 10 SERVINGS

1 pound dried Great Northern
   or navy beans

$1/2$ pound bacon, diced

1 large onion, chopped (about
   2 cups)

$1/2$ cup molasses

$1/4$ cup Dijon mustard

Kosher salt

RINSE and soak the beans according to the package directions.

COOK the bacon over medium heat in a large skillet until crisp. Remove the bacon and set aside. Discard all but about 3 tablespoons of the bacon drippings.

COOK the onion in the drippings over medium heat until soft and lightly browned, about 5 minutes.

DRAIN the beans and combine them with the bacon, onion, molasses, mustard, and 5 cups water in a medium to large slow cooker (at least 4 quarts). Cook on high for 4 to 6 hours or on low for 8 to 10 hours, until the beans are tender. Stir occasionally and add water as necessary during cooking. Season the beans with salt to taste.

Pecos Pintos

Back in the 1970s before the whole world was a mouse-click away, Min's grandfather, Lee Almy, a guy who took his beans very seriously, had pintos shipped down to Carlsbad, New Mexico, from Cortez, a small town in the prized pinto-bean-producing southwestern corner of Colorado. He flavored these superior beans simply with chili powder and salt. Min's dad, Max, adds a can of Rotel tomatoes and a leftover hambone when available and simmers them in a slow cooker.

Min's aunt Betty is a purist and cooks her pintos plain, seasoned only with salt and sometimes chopped ham. Aunt Sarah, from a long line of ranchers across Oklahoma, Texas, and New Mexico, cooks pintos the way her mama taught her—unsoaked beans and a hunk of salt pork in the pressure cooker for an hour and a half. Then she simmers them with a little fresh garlic.

Whichever way you cook them, serve with cornbread, sliced raw onion, slices of fresh jalapeño pepper, and the cheater meat of your choosing.

MAKES 8 SERVINGS

1 pound dried pinto beans

2 tablespoons vegetable oil

1 medium onion, chopped (about 1 cup)

1 cup chopped celery, with leaves

4 garlic cloves, minced

2 tablespoons chili powder

1 teaspoon ground cumin

Kosher salt

RINSE and soak the beans according to the package directions.

HEAT the oil in a large skillet over medium-high heat. Add the onion and celery and cook until tender, about 10 minutes. Stir in the garlic and cook for an additional 2 minutes.

DRAIN the beans and combine them with the vegetables, chili powder, cumin, and 6 cups of water in a medium or large slow cooker (at least 4 quarts). Cook on high for 4 to 6 hours or on low for 8 to 10 hours, until the beans are tender. Stir occasionally and add water as necessary. Season the beans with salt to taste.

Tennessee White Beans

After moving to Tennessee, R. B. discovered that his favorite baked bean cooked without molasses was actually white. Simple white beans flavored with salty local country ham are a favorite at Nashville's famous "meat and three" restaurants and at catfish joints all over Tennessee. A big slice of white onion on the side is a must. The other popular white bean garnish is a spoonful of sweet-savory chow-chow (cabbage relish). Chow-chow is available in the pickle section of Southern supermarkets.

MAKES 8 SERVINGS

1 pound dried Great Northern or navy beans

2 tablespoons vegetable oil

1 large onion, chopped (about 2 cups)

1 cup chopped celery, with leaves

1 ham bone, one 2- to 3-inch chunk of salt pork with the rind removed, 1 smoked ham hock, or 1 cup chopped country ham or baked ham scraps

Kosher salt

RINSE and soak the beans according to the package directions.

HEAT the oil in a large skillet over medium-high heat. Add the onion and celery and cook until tender, about 10 minutes.

DRAIN the beans and combine them with the vegetables, ham, and 6 cups of water in a medium or large slow cooker (at least 4 quarts). Cook on high for 4 to 6 hours or on low for 8 to 10 hours, until the beans are tender. Stir occasionally, and add water as necessary. Season the beans with salt to taste.

Cuban Black Beans

Barbecue gets along with any bean cooked with a little onion and garlic, including black beans. Cuban Black Beans with a touch of sherry are especially well suited for Cuban Fingers (page 176) with Ultimate Cheater Pork Loin (page 80). Serve the beans over rice or add some water or broth and turn them into a soup dressed with fresh parsley, chopped onion, chopped hard-cooked egg, and a dollop of yogurt or sour cream.

RINSE and soak the beans according to the package directions.

HEAT the oil in a large skillet over medium-high heat. Add the onion and celery and cook until tender, about 10 minutes. Stir in the garlic and cook for an additional 2 minutes.

DRAIN the beans and combine them with the vegetables and 6 cups of water in a medium or large slow cooker (at least 4 quarts). Cook on high for 4 to 6 hours or on low for 8 to 10 hours, until the beans are tender. Stir occasionally, and add water as necessary.

STIR in the sherry and season with salt to taste.

MAKES 8 SERVINGS

1 pound dried black beans

2 tablespoons vegetable oil

1 large onion, chopped (about 2 cups)

1 cup chopped celery, with leaves

4 garlic cloves, minced

1/4 cup dry sherry

Kosher salt

Burnt Ends Beans

When you're finished slicing and chopping a smoky beef brisket, what's left on the cutting board are the coveted crusty, juicy bits called the burnt ends. In beans, burnt ends add robust, meaty flavor just like a ham hock, a hunk of salt pork, or bacon. Here the bits of barbecue and meat juices are tossed in with canned white beans that have been doctored up with the regular barbecue sauce ingredients. We add pretty much any cheater BBQ meat scraps to canned pork and beans, too.

MAKES 8 SERVINGS

1 medium onion, chopped

2 tablespoons bacon drippings or oil

Three 15$\frac{1}{2}$-ounce cans Great Northern or navy beans, drained and rinsed

$\frac{1}{2}$ cup ketchup

$\frac{1}{2}$ cup brown sugar

2 tablespoons Worcestershire sauce

2 tablespoons cider vinegar

2 tablespoons spicy brown or Dijon mustard

2 tablespoons bottled smoke

$\frac{1}{2}$ teaspoon black pepper

$\frac{1}{2}$ cup chopped cooked beef brisket or chuck, pork butt, or chicken (plus some of the drippings)

COOK the onion in the bacon drippings in a medium skillet over medium heat until lightly browned and softened, about 8 minutes.

COMBINE the onion and the remaining ingredients in a large saucepan. Simmer over medium-low heat for about 30 minutes. Or, put everything in a medium slow cooker (at least 4 quarts). Cook on high for 2 hours or on low for 3 to 4 hours.

Cheater BBQ Slaw

There are two classic styles of slaw—vinegary and creamy mayonnaise—and probably more than a few hundred variations of each. Our cheater slaw combines the two classic styles, which you can easily push to one side or the other.

We go light on the mayo and make it sweet and tangy. If you prefer creamier, add more mayo. If you want a vinegary slaw, simply substitute water for the mayo.

See the recipe as a blueprint for your own creative preferences. We redesign it all the time by tossing in an extra ingredient or two. The usual suspects are chopped fresh parsley, fresh cilantro, shredded carrots, chopped bell pepper, bits of fresh jalapeño pepper, chopped chipotle pepper in adobo sauce, green apple chunks, sliced green onion, celery, and blue cheese crumbles.

MAKES 6 SERVINGS

1/2 cup white or cider vinegar

1/2 cup sugar

1/4 cup mayonnaise

1 teaspoon celery seed

1 teaspoon kosher salt

One 16-ounce bag slaw mix (about 8 cups lightly packed)

COMBINE the vinegar, sugar, mayonnaise, celery seed, and salt in a large mixing bowl. Blend well with a whisk or fork.

ADD the slaw mix and toss to blend. Chill before serving.

Yo Mayo Slaw

The traditional yogurt-cucumber mix that cools Middle Eastern and Indian barbecue dishes operates the same way with cheater BBQ. This slaw is a natural side to Tandoori BBQ Chicken Thighs (page 96) and Cheater Q'Balls (page 129). When we have any leftover brisket, burgers, or turkey, it gets loaded into pita pockets with as much slaw as will fit topped with whatever hot Indian chutney happens to be in Min's fridge door condiment collection at the time.

MAKES 6 SERVINGS

1 cup plain yogurt

1/2 cup mayonnaise

2 tablespoons fresh lemon juice

1 tablespoon cumin seeds

1 teaspoon kosher salt

One 16-ounce bag slaw mix

1 seedless cucumber, chopped into bite-size chunks (about 2 cups)

1/2 cup diced red onion

1/2 cup chopped fresh cilantro

COMBINE the yogurt, mayonnaise, lemon juice, cumin seeds, and salt in a large bowl. Blend well with a fork.

ADD the slaw, cucumber, and onion. Toss well to blend the vegetables with the dressing.

Gently **STIR** in the cilantro. Chill before serving.

Q-Cumbers

*T*his completely fat-free side is the perfect counterpoint to rich meat. No matter the barbecue, Q-Cumbers will expand your side dish repertoire beyond the more conventional slaws, potato salads, beans, and corn. Q-Cumbers are best icy cold.

Regular cucumbers may need their seeds removed, but the long, plastic-wrapped English/Japanese/seedless kind grown in hothouses are ready-made for thin slicing. Maybe it's psychological, but the palate-cleansing effect of fresh vinegary sweet cucumbers is extra good in hot weather. Plus, you don't have to worry about the mayonnaise issue in the heat. The jalapeños, while optional, are encouraged.

COMBINE all the ingredients in a large bowl with 1 cup of water. Cover and chill until serving time.

MAKES 8 SERVINGS

2 large seedless cucumbers, thinly sliced

1 medium sweet onion, cut into thin slivers

1 cup rice or distilled white vinegar

$1/2$ cup sugar

2 teaspoons kosher salt

$1/4$ cup chopped fresh cilantro (optional)

2 jalapeño peppers, thinly sliced (optional)

Cheater Sweet Pickles and Peños

Our good friend and food pal, Anne Byrn, author of the wildly popular Cake Mix Doctor *cookbook series and the* Dinner Doctor, *is a cheater from way back. Long before she earned advanced degrees in cake-mix doctoring, Anne was* doctoring pickles by transforming store-bought dills and sours into home-canned-style bread-and-butter pickles. Anne says cheater pickles were especially popular with her mother's generation as a "homemade" Christmas gift, and a must for serving with the Christmas country ham.

Our own sweet-hot version of cheater pickles enjoys a little heat from pickled jalapeños and tastes great with cheater meats. Pickled red jalapeños, if you can find them, are especially colorful for the holiday season. Sour pickles work best because their pungent flavor really hangs in there with all that sugar, but you can resort to regular dills in a pinch. We've had the best luck finding sours in big jars at Wal-Mart. The mustard seeds make the cheater pickles look even more homemade.

....

MAKES 4 HALF-PINT JARS

One 32-ounce jar whole sour pickles, drained

3 cups sugar

One 16-ounce jar sliced pickled jalapeño peppers or sliced hot red peppers, drained

5 garlic cloves, peeled but left whole

2 tablespoons mustard seeds

SLICE the pickles 1/4 inch thick.

COMBINE the pickles with all the remaining ingredients in a large nonaluminum (stainless steel, glass, or ceramic) mixing bowl.

COVER the bowl with plastic wrap and refrigerate for 2 to 3 days.

PACK the pickles in clean half-pint decorative jars. Seal the jars and keep refrigerated. The pickles will keep in the refrigerator for 4 to 5 months.

Sweet Corn in the Cup

Adding a little sugar to frozen vegetables is an old country kitchen trick for turning the clock back to summer. It occurred to us that revitalizing frozen corn in some sugar water is essentially a sweet brine. The other trick is plenty of butter, just like corn on the cob.

The first time we tried this was for a winter cheater barbecue party with piles of cheater brisket, pulled pork, and hot drums. Everybody loved the cute little cups of peppery sweet corn. It tasted remarkably fresh and was loads cheaper than out-of-season fresh corn or frozen ears. Corn absolutely goes with every kind of American barbecue.

MAKES 10 SERVINGS

$1/4$ cup sugar

2 pounds frozen corn, white shoepeg, yellow, or a mixture

8 tablespoons (1 stick) butter

Kosher salt and black pepper

COMBINE 2 cups of water and the sugar in a large saucepan and bring to a boil over high heat. Stir to dissolve the sugar.

ADD the corn and return to a boil. Cook for 3 to 5 minutes, stirring occasionally.

STIR in the butter and salt and pepper to taste. Serve in little cups. We use disposable clear plastic cups.

Detailed Salad
with Three Creamy Dressings

Since R. B. has expanded his blade assortment beyond an ax, a maul, and a cleaver to include a few kitchen knives, he's more than happy to wield the Santoku for diced salad vegetables. This kitchen task is best suited for the detail oriented. Around here, that would be R. B., whose T-shirt collection is always impeccably folded, stacked, and arranged by hobby. Instead of limp baby weeds, we vote for a crisp head of chilled iceberg lettuce that cuts beautifully into bite-size pieces for serving with barbecue.

MAKES 8 SERVINGS

Dressing of your choice (recipes follow)

1 medium head iceberg lettuce, cut into bite-size pieces, well chilled

2 medium tomatoes, cut into bite-size pieces

1 medium or 1/2 large seedless cucumber, thinly sliced or cut into chunks

6 radishes, sliced

2 celery ribs, sliced

1/4 cup red onion slivers

MAKE one of the following dressings. Chill.

PLACE the lettuce in a large salad bowl and toss with the dressing.

SCATTER the tomatoes, cucumber, radishes, celery, and onion over the lettuce or arrange them separately in a composed design.

······································

Cool White Dressing

Min found her inspiration for this dressing at the end of the Indian restaurant buffet. That delicious yogurt-dressed lettuce salad is crisper around here, but it's just as cooling with spicy meats. Garnish the salad with fresh cilantro and mint leaves.

MAKES ABOUT 1^1/$_4$ CUPS

1 cup yogurt
^{1}/$_4$ cup tahini
Juice of ^{1}/$_2$ lemon
1 teaspoon cumin seeds
Kosher salt to taste

COMBINE all the ingredients in a small bowl. Serve over the Detailed Salad.

······································

Engineer's Dressing

Min's dad Max, an accomplished engineer who claims two slide rules and the ability to use them, shares R. B.'s bite-size approach to salad making. His dressing of choice is creamy picante for geometrically correct iceberg lettuce and supporting vegetable elements. Garnish the salad with fresh cilantro.

MAKES ABOUT 1^1/$_2$ CUPS

1 cup mayonnaise
^{1}/$_2$ cup picante sauce
Juice of ^{1}/$_2$ lime
Kosher salt to taste

COMBINE all the ingredients in a small bowl. Serve over the Detailed Salad.

Pink Ranch Dressing

The dusky flavor of smoked paprika makes quite an impact on the usual creamy ranch. We either make this from scratch or just sprinkle the paprika into bottled ranch. A little smoked paprika is also a nice addition to any basic vinaigrette.

MAKES ABOUT 1 CUP

$1/2$ cup mayonnaise

$1/2$ cup buttermilk

2 tablespoons fresh lemon juice

1 garlic clove, mashed into a paste

2 tablespoons chopped mixed fresh herbs of your choice—chives, parsley, cilantro, thyme, oregano (or 2 teaspoons dried Italian seasoning)

1 teaspoon smoked paprika

Kosher salt and black pepper to taste

COMBINE all the ingredients in a small bowl. Serve over the Detailed Salad.

Oven-Charred-Pineapple Salads

Charring a pineapple slice steps it up from fruit salad and baked ham ornament to a more sophisticated salad sphere. Our sweet and savory charred pineapple salads are all great matches for any style of barbecued pork and run the gamut of pineapple possibilities.

Pineapple is easy to char because you're just adding some smoke and a chic look to the fruit, not cooking it. If you prefer groovy grill marks, use a ridged grill pan to sear in some lines. It takes about 3 minutes a side. For the classic charred diamond grill pattern, rotate the pineapple slices about 45 degrees on one side during the charring process. Skin and core a fresh one yourself, or find one all trimmed in the cut produce section.

MAKES 4 TO 6 SERVINGS

1 tablespoon vegetable oil

1 teaspoon bottled smoke

1 large fresh pineapple, peeled, cored, and cut into $3/4$-inch rings

$1/4$ cup sugar

HEAT the broiler. Blend the vegetable oil with the bottled smoke in a small bowl.

LAY the pineapple slices on a baking sheet. Lightly coat both sides with the oily smoke and lightly sprinkle with sugar to help caramelize the surfaces.

BROIL both sides until lightly charred, carefully flipping each slice with a spatula. Char the pineapple rings ahead of time, then refrigerate. Serve at room temperature or chilled.

Charred-Pineapple Spinach Salad

Toss together baby spinach, toasted almonds or pecans, red onion rings, pineapple chunks, and bottled sesame vinaigrette.

Charred Pineapple with Watercress and Avocado

Line a platter with fresh watercress and top with pineapple rings and avocado slices. Sprinkle with fresh chopped cilantro and drizzle with salsa mixed with bottled vinaigrette. Add a few slices of fresh jalapeño or a splash of pepper sauce to crank up the heat.

Charred Pineapple with Feta and Frisée

Top frisée (curly, slightly bitter lettuce) with pineapple chunks, crumbled feta cheese, sliced green onion, and pitted Greek olives. Drizzle with vinaigrette.

Individual Charred-Pineapple Iceberg Cups

Fill individual iceberg cups with pineapple rings. Dollop with Thousand Island dressing and sprinkle with shredded sharp Cheddar cheese. A timeless classic!

Next-Day Chef Salad with Charred Pineapple

Toss chunks of ham, Cheddar cheese, pineapple, and anything else you like with your favorite lettuce. Dress with a handy bottle of ranch from the fridge.

Cranberry Fruit Salad

Min's Cranberry Fruit Salad is the result of her crusade to bring vibrant colors and crisp textures to those brown winter meals—including plenty of the cheater pulled and chopped meats. Bright cranberries and fall fruits make a drop-dead gorgeous salad with body, color, and crunch. Smoked turkey, chicken, pork loin, and brisket are always better with a bright accessory. Freeze extra cranberries in the fall to whip this up throughout the winter.

COMBINE the cranberries, orange, ginger, and sugar in a food processor. Pulse until the orange and cranberries are uniformly small pieces, but not pureed into mush.

SPOON the cranberry mixture into a large bowl and stir in the remaining ingredients.

COVER and chill before serving.

MAKES ABOUT 10 CUPS

One 12-ounce bag fresh cranberries

1 seedless orange, with the peel, cut into chunks

1 tablespoon grated fresh ginger

3/4 cup sugar

2 medium Golden Delicious apples, chopped

2 ripe pears, chopped

2 cups seedless red grapes

Broiled Corn and Rice Salad

Min was first encouraged to make this dish when her fridge was jammed with leftover grilled corn on the cob. We liked this salad so much that now she doesn't wait for a summer corn surplus—she cheats with a bag of niblets from the freezer. Frozen white shoepeg corn and frozen baby peas are two of Min's constant freezer staples for ultraquick sides.

....
MAKES 8 SERVINGS

For the salad

One 16-ounce package frozen corn kernels, thawed

1 tablespoon vegetable oil

1 teaspoon sugar

3 cups cooked rice, chilled

2 medium tomatoes, chopped

1/3 cup chopped green onions

1/2 cup chopped celery

1/2 cup chopped fresh cilantro

For the dressing

1/3 cup olive oil

2 tablespoons Dijon mustard

1 tablespoon red wine vinegar

1 garlic clove, mashed into a paste in a garlic press or with the broad side of a knife

1/2 teaspoon kosher salt

HEAT the broiler.

PLACE the corn in a 9 x 13-inch pan or on a rimmed baking sheet. Coat the corn with the oil and sprinkle with the sugar.

BROIL the corn about 4 inches from the heat source until lightly browned in spots, 5 to 7 minutes. Stir once or twice while broiling.

COMBINE the corn, rice, tomatoes, green onions, celery, and cilantro in a large bowl.

WHISK all the dressing ingredients in a small bowl. Toss the salad with the dressing.

Cheat Sheet Tip Skip our dressing and stir up some bottled vinaigrette with a spoonful of Dijon mustard or smoked paprika.

Potato Salad

This salad uses Oven Potatoes rather than fluffy, starchy boiled potatoes. The difference is that the potatoes, browned with the help of a little oil and cooked without water, are crusty, giving the salad a new texture.

Dress the salad with either mayonnaise or vinaigrette. A little dry rub on the potatoes will add robust flavor and rusty color to the dressing, a perfect side for lightly seasoned meats and fish. If you're serving potato salad with peppery rubbed cheater BBQ, season the potatoes only with salt and skip the dry rub. One dry-rubbed menu item per meal is usually plenty.

COMBINE the salad ingredients in a large bowl and pick your dressing.

WHISK the dressing ingredients in a small bowl and toss with the salad.

MAKES 8 TO 10 SERVINGS

For the salad

Oven Potatoes (page 167)

1 cup chopped celery

1/2 cup chopped red onion or green onion

For creamy style

2/3 cup mayonnaise

1/4 cup chopped dill or sweet pickle

For vinaigrette style

1/2 cup minced fresh parsley

1/2 cup olive oil

2 tablespoons Dijon mustard

1 teaspoon red wine vinegar

Hot-Oven Cauliflower

For too long cauliflower has been confined to salad bars, vegetable medleys, and Velveeta sauces. Everything changed for us when R. B. roasted two cut-up heads in a foil packet on the grill. The transformation was amazing—instead of bland, white, and wet the florets were brown, nutty, and rich. Yes, cheese was involved. And some bacon.

A nicely browned cheater oven version is just as big a hit and has become a dinner regular. R. B. prefers the cauliflower cooked really soft, not crisp-tender, but fix it the way you like. It's good to go as is, or dressed up to suit the menu. Give our variations a try. Some are everyday good, others are fancy dinner-party style.

MAKES 6 TO 8 SERVINGS

2 cauliflower heads, cores removed, cut into about 2-inch pieces

1/4 cup olive oil

1 teaspoon kosher salt

Black pepper

HEAT the oven to 450°F.

SPREAD the cauliflower on a rimmed baking sheet. Toss with the oil and sprinkle with the salt and pepper to taste.

ROAST the cauliflower until fork-tender with browned edges, about 30 minutes. For more browning, broil the cauliflower 4 inches from the heat source for 5 to 7 minutes.

Garlic Parmesan Cauliflower

Reduce the olive oil to 2 tablespoons and add 2 tablespoons melted butter and 2 chopped garlic cloves to the cauliflower before cooking. After roasting, sprinkle with grated Parmesan and chopped fresh parsley.

Bacon Cheddar Cauliflower

Sprinkle the roasted cauliflower with shredded Cheddar and crumbled cooked bacon. Return to the oven for about 5 minutes to melt the cheese.

Swiss Cheese and Almond Cauliflower

Sprinkle the roasted cauliflower with a shredded Swiss cheese like Gruyère and toasted sliced almonds. Melt the cheese as for Bacon Cheddar Cauliflower.

Arugula and Olive Cauliflower

Spread the roasted cauliflower over a bed of arugula tossed with mustard vinaigrette. Top with chopped cured black olives.

Oven Packet Vegetables

R. B.'s childhood campout hobo packet memories have inspired many of our favorite side dishes. He's put just about every vegetable combo imaginable in a foil packet on the grill. Without added water, vegetables steam in their own juices and roast beautifully over the direct high heat of the grill. Even better and easier than the grill is the even heat of a hot oven. If there were a hobo packet merit badge, R. B. would have definitely earned it.

MAKES 4 SERVINGS

1 pound of vegetables per packet, cut into slices, wedges, or chunks as necessary (try Brussels sprouts, broccoli florets, carrots, parsnips, sweet potatoes, winter or summer squash, fingerling or waxy potatoes, fennel, turnips, beets, cabbage, onions, bell pepper, eggplant, tomatoes)

2 tablespoons olive oil, vegetable oil, or butter

Kosher salt and black pepper

Optional seasonings include cheater dry rubs, smoked paprika, dried herbs, minced fresh garlic, smoked salts, and seasoning blends

HEAT the oven to 450°F.

PLACE the vegetables in a single layer on a large piece of heavy-duty foil or in a foil 10 x 12-inch roasting or lasagna pan. Toss them with the oil, salt and pepper to taste, and whatever seasonings you want. Seal the foil tightly or cover the pan tightly with foil.

PLACE the packet directly on the oven rack or on a baking sheet. Roast for 30 to 45 minutes. When you can smell their aroma, the vegetables will be tender and cooked.

For extra browning, OPEN the foil packet and continue roasting until lightly browned, 5 to 10 minutes.

Oven Potatoes

If you want potatoes with more crust, cook them in an open roasting pan. Cut 2 pounds (about 8 medium) waxy potatoes into bite-size pieces and put them in a roasting pan. Drizzle with about 3 tablespoons of oil and stir to coat the potatoes. Sprinkle with salt and, if you like, either smoked paprika or about 2 tablespoons of dry rub. Bake at 450°F for 45 minutes to 1 hour. Stir occasionally. Serve oven potatoes hot, warm, or chilled in Potato Salad (page 163).

Get Along Roasted Roots

A spirited family debate one holiday season over the merits of sweet versus white potatoes prompted this compromise—colorful root vegetables all coexisting nicely in one big happy roasting pan. Frozen pearl onions are easy to use right out of the bag and make the dish look extra fancy. You can cook the vegetables early in the day and stick them back in the oven to warm before dinner with whatever's cooking. These are delicious sprinkled with smoked paprika.

MAKES 8 SERVINGS

5 medium red potatoes

3 medium sweet potatoes

6 medium carrots

2 medium onions, cut into wedges, or $1/2$ pound frozen pearl onions

$1/4$ cup olive oil

Kosher salt and black pepper

Chopped fresh parsley

HEAT the oven to 400°F.

PEEL the vegetables and cut them into 2-inch pieces.

TOSS all the vegetables in the oil in a large roasting pan. Season with salt and pepper to taste.

COOK for about 1 hour or until the vegetables are lightly browned and tender. Garnish with a sprinkle of parsley.

Micro-Broiled Winter Squash

The key to enjoying dense winter squash more often is a time-saving ten or so minutes in the microwave. By cooking them first, you avoid the anxiety and danger of hacking a sturdy squash or your finger in half. Or, look for packages of ready-to-cook precut and peeled squash in the supermarket.

After cooking, the other trick is to scoop the flesh into a casserole where it's easy to char evenly under the broiler in a couple minutes. This way no one has to negotiate an unwieldy squash boat, and everyone gets as much or as little as they want. Make the casserole ahead and you'll be glad come dinnertime.

The trio of squash sauces shows how well squash gets along with a full range of sweet to savory flavors. One sauce is traditional—buttery and sweet with pecans. The second is a sweet-savory exotic beauty blending spicy chutney, dried cranberries, and almonds. The third, a savory tomato, mysteriously brings out the sweetness of the squash without overpowering it. Serve all three sauces with any squash combo and watch everyone duke it out for a favorite.

....

MAKES 6 SERVINGS

2 medium winter squash (about 2 pounds each)— Hubbard, butternut, acorn, turban, spaghetti, or buttercup

$1/4$ cup olive oil or $1/2$ stick butter, melted (or more, to taste)

Kosher salt

Squash sauce (recipes follow)

PIERCE the skin of the squash in a few places with the tip of a knife. Place in a microwave-safe dish.

MICROWAVE one squash at a time on high for 10 to 12 minutes. The squash skin should feel soft, but not mushy. Let the squash cool for about 5 minutes.

HEAT the broiler. Butter a large ovenproof casserole.

CUT each squash in half and scoop out the seeds. With a big spoon, scoop the flesh into the prepared dish. Drizzle the olive oil over the top and sprinkle with salt to taste. Broil on high 4 inches from the heat source until lightly charred to your liking, about 5 minutes.

SERVE with the squash sauce of your choice.

······································

Sweet Squash Sauce

4 tablespoons ($^1/_2$ stick) butter
$^1/_2$ cup pecans
$^1/_2$ cup applesauce
$^1/_2$ cup brown sugar
$^1/_2$ teaspoon cinnamon (optional)
Pinch of kosher salt

Melt the butter in a small saucepan. Stir in the pecans and cook over medium heat until lightly toasted, about 3 minutes. Stir in the remaining ingredients. Spoon the sauce over the warm squash.

······································

Chutney Squash Sauce

4 tablespoons ($^1/_2$ stick) butter
$^1/_4$ cup sliced almonds
$^1/_2$ cup Major Grey's mango chutney
$^1/_4$ cup dried cranberries
1 tablespoon grated fresh orange zest
Pinch of kosher salt

Melt the butter in a small saucepan. Stir in the almonds and cook over medium heat until lightly toasted, about 2 minutes. Stir in the remaining ingredients. Spoon the sauce over the warm squash.

. . . .

Savory Squash Sauce

4 tablespoons (^{1}/2 stick) butter
1 small onion, chopped
2 garlic cloves, minced
One 14^1/2-ounce can diced tomatoes, drained
2 teaspoons sugar
^{1}/2 teaspoon Italian seasoning
Pinch of kosher salt

Melt the butter in a small saucepan. Stir in the onion and cook over medium heat for about 5 minutes. Stir in the garlic and cook for an additional 2 minutes, or until the onion is soft and beginning to brown. Stir in the remaining ingredients. Spoon the sauce over the warm squash.

Cheater Fajita Onions

We're sweet onion junkies and whenever beef is on the grill, so are a pile of onion slices. At first, we just served them with Mexican fajita feasts, but then quickly found that their sweet, salty, smoky, soft, and crisp qualities turned plain old burgers into chopped steak and added richness and depth to all kinds of meats.

Now that we've become cheaters, so have the onions. Charred in the oven, these smoky sweet onions are just what cheater brisket needs on the side. Days later diced leftover onions end up in all kinds of meals like a weekend fridge scramble, hash browns, baked beans, and green beans.

Georgia's Vidalia onions are a big thing in Tennessee, and we're seeing more and more varieties of sweet onions from Texas and Washington. Take your pick, but any yellow or white onion will do the job.

MAKES 6 TO 8 SERVINGS

4 large Vidalia or other sweet onions
1/4 cup vegetable or olive oil
2 tablespoons bottled smoke
Kosher salt

HEAT the oven to 450°F.

CUT the onions into 1/2-inch slices, separate them into rings, and place them in a large roasting pan. Toss with the oil, bottled smoke, and salt to taste.

ROAST for 20 minutes, or until the onions are soft and golden brown.

Skillet Onions

Make these when you're not cooking for a crowd or don't want to turn on the oven. Cut 2 large sweet onions into 1/2-inch slices. Heat 2 tablespoons of vegetable or olive oil in a heavy skillet. Add the onions and cook, stirring constantly, for 3 to 5 minutes. Stir in a tablespoon of bottled smoke, a pinch of salt, and a pinch of sugar. Cook for an additional 2 to 3 minutes. The onions can be made ahead and reheated in the skillet just before serving.

Asian Greens

Lots of barbecue joints in Tennessee do country-style vegetables other than coleslaw, barbecued beans, and potato salad. One of our favorites is a big pile of turnip greens doused with hot pepper vinegar to go with a side of pork ribs. We think vegetables are a critical counterbalance to rich smoky barbecued meats. Same goes with Asian barbecue. Swap the collards and turnip greens for bok choy or Napa cabbage flavored with garlic, ginger, and soy sauce. Serve this with Filipino Adobo-Q Chicken (page 94) and a big pile of fluffy jasmine rice.

COOK the onion, garlic, and ginger in the oil over medium-high heat in a large skillet for 8 to 10 minutes.

FOLD in the greens and cook, stirring, until wilted, about 5 minutes.

STIR in the soy sauce and sprinkle the greens with sesame seeds just before serving.

MAKES 4 TO 6 SERVINGS

1 medium onion, chopped

2 garlic cloves, chopped

2 tablespoons grated fresh ginger

3 tablespoons peanut or vegetable oil

1 pound Asian greens such as bok choy or Napa cabbage, cut into 2-inch pieces (about 8 cups)

2 to 3 tablespoons soy sauce

1 tablespoon sesame seeds, toasted (see page 67)

CHAPTER 8

Two-Timing Cheater Recipes

Cuban Fingers

Part of the fun of Nashville is the occasional encounter with the music community—Martina at the supermarket, Keith at the sushi bar, Kenny at the gym, Wynonna doing lunch, or Mr. Prine waiting in the school car line. Nashville is good about giving Grammy winners, hit songwriters, and all who keep the music playing plenty of space for living their regular lives.

Over at Min's, we enjoy the occasional drop-in visit by the Malo posse, the charming sons of velvet-voiced Raul Malo. We shoot the breeze about Dad's latest album, fast cars, and food. No luck getting any Cuban secret family recipes, but the boys have kindly offered Dad's autograph on our Mavericks and Raul Malo CDs.

Listening to Raul gets us hungry for Cuban Fingers, Miami's favorite crusty pressed sandwiches. We fill them with Ultimate Cheater Pork Loin, or sometimes leftover cheater brisket or beef round roast. Cuban bread is extra crisp on the outside and very tender on the inside, so it's easy to flatten. Cut the sandwiches into neat fingers for parties.

MAKES 4 TO 6 SERVINGS

- 1 large loaf (20 to 24 inches long) Cuban or French bread
- 4 tablespoons ($^1/_2$ stick) butter, melted
- $^1/_2$ pound thinly sliced Ultimate Cheater Pork Loin (page 80), any cheater brisket, or One-Hour Rump or Round Roast (page 118)
- $^1/_2$ pound thinly sliced deli ham
- Dill pickle chips
- $^1/_2$ pound thinly sliced Swiss cheese

CUT the bread into four equal pieces with a serrated knife. Slice each piece in half lengthwise. Brush the insides with butter and place them on a baking sheet.

TOAST the bread, buttered side up, under a broiler or in a toaster oven until lightly browned.

PILE the four bottoms with the pork loin, ham, pickles, and cheese. Add the tops and flatten the sandwiches with the bottom of a skillet, a spatula, or your hand.

TOAST the sandwiches in a skillet or sandwich press over medium heat until lightly browned on both sides and the cheese is melted. Press the sandwiches occasionally while cooking. Cut into 1- to 2-inch fingers.

Posole

Posole (pronounced poh-SO-lay), a Mexican soup adopted by northern New Mexico, is all about the hominy—bloated corn kernels softened with an alkali. Purists will cook their own from dried corn, but canned hominy is a terrific pantry staple for making a quick soup. Pork is the traditional meat for posole, but we like it with cheater chicken and beef as well. Serve posole in big bowls with a side of thinly shredded cabbage, diced onions, chopped tomato, a crisp tostado to crumble in the soup, and a lime wedge. Punch it up with a little hot sauce. Every time we make a batch, Min always says we should make this more often.

COOK the onion in the oil in a soup pot over medium heat until soft and lightly browned, about 5 minutes.

STIR in the remaining soup ingredients along with 2 cups water and simmer for about 30 minutes.

PASS bowls of garnishes at the table for everyone to help themselves.

....

MAKES 6 TO 8 SERVINGS

For the soup

1 large onion, chopped

2 tablespoons vegetable oil

3 cups chopped leftover cheater meat like pork shoulder, beef brisket, chuck, or chicken

One 28-ounce can diced tomatoes

Two 14$^{1}/_{2}$-ounce cans chicken broth

One 30-ounce can white or yellow hominy, drained

1 tablespoon chili powder

For the toppings

Lime wedges, shredded cabbage, chopped onion, sprigs of fresh cilantro, avocado slices, and crumbled fried corn tortillas

Choucroute Garni

*G*ood freezer management makes it so much easier to get away with two-timing. When the freezer door won't close, we know it's time for a couple bags of sauerkraut for an Alsatian choucroute (pronounced shoo-KROOT) garni.

A French peasant dish from the Alsace region, choucroute garni means sauerkraut "garnished" with an abundance of pork products, or occasionally goose or duck. It's the perfect freezer purge for using up all manner of cheater pork plus any sausages, bacon, or ham bones. Whatever you find in there will pretty much work with this dish.

Choucroute (the sauerkraut) is traditionally slow-baked in a heavy casserole with slab bacon or a ham hock, carrots, onion, garlic, apple, and wine or beer. The seasoning mix depends on the cook (or the pantry), but usually includes juniper berries, bay leaves, cloves, black or white pepper, even cumin and coriander seeds. The sausages, ham, and other meats are added near the end of cooking.

Get the bagged or jarred sauerkraut for the freshest taste. While the sauerkraut turns French in the oven, thaw the trove of frozen meats. A fruity, dry Alsatian Riesling is traditional for both cooking and drinking. French and German beers are also a good match. To complete the meal, add boiled potatoes and a green salad.

MAKES 10 SERVINGS

Two 1-pound bags sauerkraut, drained

2 tablespoons bacon drippings or a few slices of bacon, diced

2 medium onions, chopped

2 medium carrots, chopped

1 Granny Smith apple, peeled, cored, and grated

1 garlic clove, minced

One or two 14$\frac{1}{2}$-ounce cans chicken broth

2 cups dry white wine or beer

1 ham hock, fresh or store-bought smoked

1 bay leaf

1 teaspoon juniper berries

1 teaspoon coriander seeds

$\frac{1}{2}$ teaspoon black peppercorns

$\frac{1}{2}$ teaspoon cumin seeds

$\frac{1}{4}$ teaspoon whole cloves

Kosher salt and black pepper to taste

4 to 5 pounds of cooked meat—choose a variety, such as sausages, hot dogs, ham chunks, any cheater pork, and Five-Star Duck Legs (page 103)

Dijon mustard

Boiled potatoes

HEAT the oven to 325°F.

RINSE the sauerkraut under running water and drain thoroughly; set aside.

In a large Dutch oven (6 to 8 quarts), **HEAT** the bacon drippings. (If starting with sliced bacon, cook it to render the fat. Set aside the bacon, leaving the drippings.)

ADD the onions and cook over medium heat until softened, about 8 minutes.

ADD the carrots, apple, and garlic and cook for an additional 5 minutes.

ADD the sauerkraut, cooked bacon (if using), chicken broth, wine, ham hock, and the remaining seasonings. Bring the pot to a simmer.

COVER the pot and bake for 2 hours. Remove the pot from the oven and tuck the cooked meats into the choucroute. Stir in additional chicken broth if it seems dry.

COVER and bake for an additional 30 minutes. Serve with Dijon mustard and boiled potatoes.

Asian Noodle Bowls

No matter how much you like to cook, everyone gets stuck in a rut. When you find yourself making the same old things, it's time to cook out of your comfort zone. For us, this means a trip to any international market where one step inside we remember how much there still is to learn. The good news is that walking the aisles of the unfamiliar unlocks the secrets to many of the ingredients in our favorite restaurant dishes. The greens in the produce section alone will keep us busy for a year.

We can't shop when we're hungry, so first we eat. Thankfully, the Vietnamese noodle bowls right next door energize and inspire our international shopping trips.

Vietnamese noodle bowls are filled with contradictions in complete agreement—hot and cold, crunchy and soft, sweet and sour, rich and light. The bowls of warm thin noodles, cool leafy lettuce, bean sprouts, and herbs topped with any meat or seafood you like are perfect for leftover cheater meat. The sweet/salty/spicy dressing may appear way too complex for home cooking. It's not. The international market has everything you need.

Cooking out of your comfort zone will help you dissect the components and flavors of unfamiliar foods. Even if cooking Vietnamese at home sounds daunting, give this a try with leftover cheater meat just for the fun of better understanding how opposites get along.

....

MAKES 4 TO 6 SERVINGS

For the Noodle Bowl Sauce

3/4 cup rice vinegar

1/4 cup sugar

2 tablespoons nuoc mam (Vietnamese/Thai fish sauce)

2 teaspoons toasted sesame oil

2 teaspoons Asian hot chili sauce (sriracha)

1 tablespoon grated fresh ginger (optional)

For the Noodle Bowls

1 package (about 1 pound) rice vermicelli

1 head leaf lettuce, torn into pieces

1/2 pound pea pods, blanched for 1 minute, covered, in the microwave

1/2 pound bean sprouts

1 small bunch fresh cilantro sprigs

1 small bunch fresh Thai or other basil

1 1/2 pounds leftover cheater beef, pork, chicken, or turkey, cut into chunks

1 bunch green onions, halved lengthwise and cut into 1-inch pieces

2 fresh jalapeño peppers, sliced

1/2 cup chopped unsalted peanuts

COMBINE all the Noodle Bowl Sauce ingredients with 1/4 cup water in a medium bowl and set aside.

COOK the noodles according to package directions in boiling salted water. Drain and rinse with cold water.

In individual serving bowls, LAYER the lettuce, noodles, pea pods, bean sprouts, and sprigs of cilantro and basil.

ARRANGE the meat on top. Sprinkle with the green onions, jalapeños, and peanuts, to taste.

DRIZZLE each serving with the Noodle Bowl Sauce. Serve with fish sauce, hot sauce, and soy sauce at the table.

Goulash Soup

Goulash may not sound flashy or stylish, but it offers lots of room for creative leftover cheating out of the vegetable crisper drawer or the freezer. Cheater beef chuck is the delicious traditional choice for goulash, but Ultimate Cheater Pulled Chicken (page 85) or Ultimate Cheater Pulled Pork (page 54) make a respectable soup.

The secret to goulash is the combination of sweet slow-cooked caramelized onions with traditional pungent Hungarian paprika or a little Spanish smoked paprika. Keep most of the paprika on the sweet side, or the soup will go from zero to sixty too fast for tender palates. Serve with a loaf of good crusty bread.

....

MAKES 8 SERVINGS

4 medium onions, chopped (about 4 cups)

2 tablespoons vegetable oil

3 to 4 cups chopped leftover cheater meat like pork shoulder, beef brisket, chuck, or chicken

Two 14^1/2-ounce cans chicken or beef broth

^{1}/4 cup Hungarian paprika (mostly sweet, with some hot if you like)

2 bay leaves

4 medium potatoes such as russet or Yukon gold, peeled and diced

5 medium carrots, peeled and sliced

Kosher salt to taste

COOK the onions in the oil in a heavy soup pot over low heat until very soft and lightly browned, stirring occasionally, about 30 minutes.

STIR in the remaining ingredients along with 1 quart water. Simmer until the potatoes and carrots are tender, 30 to 45 minutes.

TWO-TIMING CHEAT SHEET

As you can imagine, we keep a steady supply of brisket, pulled pork, and chicken in the freezer. R. B. is our resident expert in leftover cuisine. Once he decided that everything goes with everything, especially with melted cheese, the cheater options exploded. Here are some of his two-timing favorites for a quick meal from the toaster oven or a full-blown brunch or dinner.

WEEKEND HASH—Cook up leftover cheater meat and packet potatoes with onions in a skillet until crusty. Serve topped with fried eggs and salsa.

STUFFED BAKERS—Fill baked potatoes with leftover cheater meat warmed with a little barbecue sauce. Top with shredded cheese and chopped fresh onion.

NACHOS GRANDE—Top tortilla chips or corn tostada shells with cheater meat and cheese. Broil until the cheese is melted. Serve with nacho fixings like sliced jalapeños, black olive slices, salsa, sour cream, sliced green onions, and chopped fresh cilantro.

(continued)

TWO-TIMING CHEATER RECIPES

ULTIMATE CHILI—We guarantee that your chili recipe, any chili recipe, will taste fifty times better made with chopped cheater brisket or chuck instead of ground beef. Be sure to throw in the leftover brisket broth.

TACO WAGON TACOS—The Nashville taco wagons serve the best very simple Mexican tacos. To make them at home, crisp up any cheater meat in a skillet. Pile the meat in warmed soft corn or flour tortillas. Top with finely diced white onion, chopped fresh cilantro, chunks of ripe avocado, and a squeeze of fresh lime juice. That's it. Add a bit of green salsa to stay with the color scheme. No cheese, no beans, no tomato.

Tortilla Soup

R. B. has discovered from his guitar teacher, Wayne Avers, that playing music is a lot like cooking. A solid background in fundamental scales and chords is the key ingredient for intuitive playing. As with cooking, the more you can take advantage of a basic, well-stocked pantry, the better prepared you are for cooking on the fly.

For tortilla soup, a regular two-timing favorite, we have on hand onions, potatoes, celery, and carrots and cans of tomatoes, beans, and broth. With these ingredients, some seasonings, and some cheater meat, you've got dinner. Go lighter on the chipotle peppers for a milder flavor.

COOK the onion in the oil in a soup pot over medium heat until soft and lightly browned, about 5 minutes.

STIR in the remaining soup ingredients. Simmer the soup for about 30 minutes.

PASS bowls of garnishes at the table for everyone to help themselves.

MAKES 6 TO 8 SERVINGS

For the soup

1 large onion, chopped

2 tablespoons vegetable oil

1 large green pepper, chopped

5 medium carrots, peeled and sliced into thin rounds

3 cups chopped leftover cheater meat like pork shoulder, beef, chuck, or chicken

One 28-ounce can diced tomatoes

Two 14$\frac{1}{2}$-ounce cans chicken broth

$\frac{1}{4}$ cup minced chipotle peppers in adobo sauce

$\frac{1}{2}$ cup chopped green chiles, frozen, or 2 small cans (optional)

1 teaspoon ground cumin

For the toppings

Lime wedges, avocado slices, crumbled fried corn tortillas, sprigs of fresh cilantro, and sour cream

Asian Tortilla Wraps

Barbecue has lots of definitions, but what it really means to us is lots of leftover piles of meat for new and different dishes. Barbecue dishes can be as versatile as you want them to be—they don't have to include slaw and beans. Pulled pork that's been lightly seasoned and smoked can go in any direction. R. B. is adamant about crisping the cooked meat in a hot skillet first. The meat takes on a new texture that's great for sandwiches, tacos, and brunch hash. Here, soft tacos made with any cheater meat take on Asian flavors with a simple sweet-hot peanut BBQ sauce and some fresh fixings.

MAKES 6 TO 8 SERVINGS

2 pounds any leftover cheater meat, shredded or chopped

Juice of 1 or 2 limes

Min Dynasty BBQ Sauce

1 cup bottled plum sauce

$1/4$ cup Asian hot chili sauce (sriracha)

$1/2$ cup chopped unsalted roasted peanuts

Taco fixings

Small flour tortillas, warmed

1 medium seedless cucumber, peeled and thinly sliced

1 medium red onion, cut into thin slivers

Fresh mint leaves

Fresh cilantro leaves

HEAT the cheater meat in a large skillet over medium heat until warm and a little crusty. Squeeze fresh lime juice over the meat.

COMBINE all the sauce ingredients in a small bowl and blend well.

SERVE the warm meat and sauce with all the taco fixings for everyone to help themselves.

Ranch-Style BBQ Cornbread Pie

Ranch Style® Beans are Min's number one foolproof side dish for instant satisfaction every time. She says that if Andy Warhol had been a Texan, the Ranch Style® Beans can would hang in museums throughout the world. The chili pintos' unmistakable label dressed in basic black with bright white Western lettering and yellow and red accents is as common a sight in Southwestern pantries as Campbell's tomato soup ever was. These well-seasoned beans make an "appetite pleasin'" homey cornbread casserole with any leftover cheater meat.

HEAT the oven to 400°F. Grease a 2-quart casserole with cooking spray.

COOK the onion in 2 tablespoons of the oil in a large skillet over medium heat until softened and lightly browned, 5 to 8 minutes.

STIR in the beans and the meat. Cook until heated through, about 2 minutes. Pour the mixture into the casserole.

COMBINE the cornmeal, baking powder, and salt in a medium mixing bowl. Add the milk and remaining 2 tablespoons oil. Stir in the cheese and jalapeños, if using.

MAKES 6 SERVINGS

1 medium onion, chopped

1/4 cup vegetable oil

Two 15-ounce cans Ranch Style® Beans

2 cups chopped leftover cheater meat like pulled pork, beef brisket, chuck, or chicken

1 cup cornmeal

1 1/2 teaspoons baking powder

1/2 teaspoon kosher salt

3/4 cup milk

1 cup shredded Cheddar cheese

2 fresh jalapeño peppers, seeded and diced (optional)

For the toppings (optional)

Shredded iceberg lettuce, chopped tomatoes, sliced green onions, diced avocado, and salsa

POUR the cornbread mixture over the meat and beans. Leave a few spots around the edges for the chili mixture to bubble through and for the steam to escape.

BAKE for 35 to 40 minutes, until the cornbread is lightly browned. Serve with toppings as desired.

Note: You can substitute 1 cup self-rising cornmeal mix for the cornmeal, baking powder, and salt.

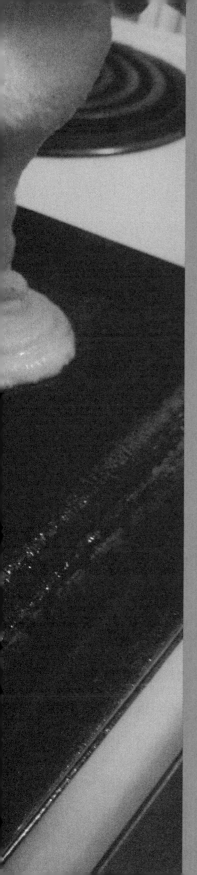

CHAPTER 9

Cheater Breads and Desserts

Skillet Cornbread

Other than a soft bun or white bread, cornbread is the choice for barbecue. Min has been making it so long she only uses the recipe in her head. After years of working with the test kitchen staff of Martha White, the historic Nashville flour and cornmeal company, and writing the live radio commercials for Martha White's Friday night segment of the Grand Ole Opry, who needs a recipe? The key, of course, is self-rising cornmeal mix.

MAKES 8 SERVINGS

4 tablespoons bacon drippings
   or vegetable oil

1 large egg

3/4 cup milk or buttermilk (plus
   water as needed)

1 cup cornmeal

1/4 cup all-purpose flour

1 1/2 teaspoons baking powder

1/2 teaspoon kosher salt

Southerners prefer white cornmeal (made with white corn) to yellow. So do Rhode Islanders, as R. B. likes to point out, where the native white corn johnnycakes are as ancient as their close cousins, Southern hot water hoecakes. Either way, white and yellow are interchangeable and basically a regional preference, like white and brown eggs.

Don't get hung up on color. For cornbread, it's all about crust and batter. First, the best crust comes only from a well-seasoned black iron skillet preheated with bacon drippings or oil. When the batter hits the pan, POW! It sizzles.

Second, the batter must be creamy and pourable. If your batter is thick and dense, add more liquid, because you want the batter to slide to the edges of the pan with ease. Cornmeal absorbs quite a lot of liquid, and even a shot of water can loosen things up. Get the feel of good cornbread batter, and crumbly, dry cornbread will be a thing of the past.

Now, about the balance of outside crust to inside moisture. For Min, the finest cornbread is an inch thick and a mile wide. Most 2-cup recipes baked in an 8- or 10-inch skillet are just too tall, denying the cornbread its rightful ratio of crust. Min uses about 1 1/2 cups of cornmeal mix for a 12-inch skillet and only about a cup for a 10-inch.

Sugar is also an issue that divides cornbread camps. The most common cornbread recipes and mixes are often half flour and half cornmeal, with a heavy dose of sweetness. We're in the other camp, using very little sugar (or none at all) in skillet cornbread. It's just a matter of taste.

If you live in the land of self-rising cornmeal mix, get acquainted with it and use *it to replace the plain cornmeal, flour, leavening, and salt. It's the best way to go. If not, and you don't have a relative to send you some, give this a try. Always serve cornbread flipped out of the pan with the beautiful browned crust faceup.*

Whatever you do, invest in a good cast-iron skillet. It will bring your family generations of top-notch cornbread.

HEAT the oven to 450°F. Grease a 10-inch cast-iron skillet with 1 tablespoon of the drippings. Heat the skillet in the oven for about 10 minutes.

COMBINE the egg, milk, and remaining 3 tablespoons of bacon drippings in a medium mixing bowl.

STIR in the cornmeal, flour, baking powder, and salt. The batter should be creamy and pourable like pancake batter. If it seems too thick or thickens while the oven and skillet heat, stir in a little water.

POUR the batter into the hot skillet. Bake for 15 to 18 minutes, until the edges look deep golden brown and the top is firm to the touch.

Note: You can substitute $1\frac{1}{4}$ cups self-rising cornmeal mix for the cornmeal, all-purpose flour, baking powder, and salt.

. . . .

Corn Cakes

You can also make corn cakes with this same batter, a popular carrier for a pile of pulled pork. Heat a greased griddle over medium heat. For each corn cake, pour about $\frac{1}{4}$ cup of the batter onto the hot griddle. Flip when the edges are dry and the bottom side is a deep golden brown. The recipe will make about 12.

BAKING CHEAT SHEET

SELF-RISING FLOUR AND SELF-RISING CORNMEAL

Self-rising flour and self-rising cornmeal are Min's most important cheater baking essentials. These popular Southern baking products are perfect combinations of all-purpose flour (or cornmeal), leavening, and salt for baking biscuits, quick breads and cakes, and cornbread.

Generations ago, these modern self-rising conveniences changed the way Southerners bake. In the rural South, biscuits and cornbread were baked every day, and ready-to-go blends eased the burden on the home cook with consistent, time-saving result. It's easy to overlook them today as they compete for shelf space with product-specific mixes for biscuits, muffins, cornbreads, pancakes, and other quick breads. With bags of self-rising flour and cornmeal, you can eliminate the rest. They're the Cheater Basic Dry Rubs of baking.

Corn Light Bread

Corn Light Bread, a favorite barbecue side in middle Tennessee, breaks all the Southern cornbread rules. It's loaded with flour and sugar and it's baked in a loaf pan. Why sweet cornbread with barbecue? Our guess is that sweet-sauced barbecue calls for a sweeter bread, just like the customary pairing of a sweet wine with a sweet dessert. Anything not sweet enough just tastes sour. Judging how most of the country prefers sweet cornbread, this may be the one that tastes the most like home.

HEAT the oven to 375°F. Grease a 9 x 5 x 3-inch loaf pan.

STIR the cornmeal, flour, sugar, baking powder, and salt in a large mixing bowl.

ADD the egg, buttermilk, and vegetable oil. Stir until well blended. The batter should be thick, but creamy and pourable. If the batter seems too thick, add a tablespoon or two of water.

POUR the batter into the loaf pan. Bake for 45 minutes, until golden brown.

COOL the bread for 5 to 10 minutes in the pan, then remove from the pan and cool on a wire rack. Store tightly wrapped in aluminum foil.

Note: You can substitute 2 cups self-rising cornmeal mix and 1 cup self-rising flour for the cornmeal, all-purpose flour, baking powder, and salt.

MAKES 1 LOAF

2 cups cornmeal

1 cup all-purpose flour

$^{1}/_{2}$ cup sugar

1 tablespoon baking powder

$^{1}/_{2}$ teaspoon kosher salt

1 large egg

$1^{1}/_{2}$ cups buttermilk

$^{1}/_{3}$ cup vegetable oil

CHEATER BREADS AND DESSERTS

Loaded Cornbread

*L*oaded Cornbread is the cornbread for a crowd and essential for a big barbecue. *Dense and moist with Cheddar cheese, cream-style corn, and buttermilk, it can be baked in advance and cut into neat squares. Unlike traditional skillet cornbread that's best eaten hot out of the oven, Loaded Cornbread travels well and tastes fine at room temperature.*

The jalapeños are up to you. Substitute a chopped fresh mild green chile or even a can of them. The other substitution is yogurt for buttermilk. Again, if the batter seems too thick, add a little water.

··

MAKES 16 SERVINGS

One 14³/4-ounce can cream-style corn

1¹/2 cups buttermilk

1 large egg

¹/4 cup vegetable oil

2¹/2 cups cornmeal

¹/2 cup all-purpose flour

1 tablespoon baking powder

1 teaspoon kosher salt

2 cups shredded Cheddar cheese

3 fresh jalapeño peppers, seeded and diced

HEAT the oven to 400°F. Grease a 9 x 13-inch baking pan.

COMBINE the corn, buttermilk, egg, and oil in a large mixing bowl.

ADD the cornmeal, flour, baking powder, and salt. Stir until well blended. Fold in the cheese and the jalapeños.

BAKE for 30 to 35 minutes, until golden brown.

Note: You can substitute 3 cups self-rising cornmeal mix for the cornmeal, all-purpose flour, baking powder, and salt.

Cookie Sheet S'Mores

*T*hese just might be the first s'mores you'll ever eat that don't come dipped in ashes. And it takes only eight marshmallows to make eight s'mores because none are sacrificed in the fire. A quick dip in bottled smoke and a sprinkling of Cheater Smoked Sweet Salt are the other secrets to bringing adult sophistication to this kiddie camp classic. Mix and match cookies and graham crackers with different chocolates and candy bars. The marshmallows will burn in the oven, so watch them carefully and don't leave your post.

Cookie Sheet S'mores don't need to be served hot. We were surprised at a winter birthday barbecue for Min's daughter, Elsa, when we laid out a platter and guests of all ages kept sneaking just one more s'more until they were gone. Use a variety of smallish store-bought cookies so everyone can try different combinations.

....

MAKES 8 SERVINGS

8 flat cookies such as peanut
   butter, chocolate,
   gingersnaps, or sugar

2 milk or dark chocolate bars,
   1½ to 2 ounces each

Bottled smoke

8 marshmallows

Cheater Smoked Sweet Salt
   (page 49)

HEAT the oven to 450°F.

PLACE the cookies on a baking sheet. Top each with a piece of chocolate.

BAKE for 1 minute or so to soften the chocolate. Remove from the oven.

POUR a small amount of bottled smoke into a small dish. Dip each marshmallow lightly in the bottled smoke. Place one marshmallow on its side on the chocolate.

BAKE in the 450°F oven or broil 6 to 8 inches from the heat source for 3 to 4 minutes, until the marshmallows are lightly browned and puffed.

REMOVE from the oven and sprinkle each cookie with the sweet salt while the marshmallows are hot.

SERVE immediately while hot or later at room temperature. You can also rewarm the cookies in the oven briefly to soften the marshmallow. Again, watch them carefully and don't leave them unattended, as they burn easily.

Peanut Butter S'Mores

Start with chocolate or peanut butter cookies. Replace the chocolate with a peanut butter cup or place a dollop of peanut butter on top of the softened chocolate before adding the marshmallow.

Coconut S'Mores

Start with chocolate cookies and place a generous pinch of shredded coconut on top of the softened chocolate before adding the marshmallow.

Peppermint S'Mores

Start with chocolate cookies and replace the chocolate bars with Peppermint Patties.

Cheater Smoked Dessert Sauces

*I*t may sound odd, but bottled smoke is the secret ingredient in our three fabulously easy dessert sauces—chocolate, caramel, and marshmallow. A tiny amount of smoke adds shocking depth to these everyday ingredients. Use the cheater dessert sauces whenever you want to dazzle an audience. We guarantee that dinner conversation will escalate when you present dishes of ice cream with one, two, or all three mingled together with toasted nuts and a light sprinkle of Cheater Smoked Sweet Salt (page 49).

Deep Smoked Chocolate Sauce

Remember that chocolate is made by roasting, so why not combine a few drops of smoke with supermarket chocolate chips? That got us thinking about coffee, which also matches well with smoke and chocolate. Instant coffee is possibly the bottled smoke of coffee. Way before designer coffeehouses, instant coffee was the hot ticket. It's just dehydrated coffee in a granulated form. It may not be your favorite for sipping, but it is a mighty useful pantry staple for adding undiluted coffee flavor to desserts.

MAKES ABOUT 2 CUPS

1 cup heavy cream

One 12-ounce bag semisweet chocolate chips

1/2 cup light corn syrup

1 teaspoon bottled smoke

1 teaspoon vanilla extract

BRING the cream to a boil in a small saucepan. Remove from the heat and add the chocolate, corn syrup, bottled smoke, and vanilla. Stir until smooth.

Mochacheater Sauce

Add 2 tablespoons of instant coffee powder to the Deep Smoked Chocolate Sauce.

Cheater Peppermint Fudge Sauce

Add a teaspoon of peppermint extract to the sauce.

Smoky Caramel Sauce

*S*urprise, a touch of bottled smoke is the easy route to burnt sugar flavor in caramel sauce. This melt-and-stir cheater sauce eliminates the intimidating and time-consuming step of caramelizing sugar—cooking white sugar slowly in a skillet until it turns toasty brown.

....

MAKES ABOUT 2 CUPS

8 tablespoons (1 stick) butter

1 cup brown sugar

$1/2$ cup heavy cream

$1/4$ cup corn syrup

$1/2$ teaspoon bottled smoke

1 teaspoon vanilla extract

COMBINE all the ingredients in a small saucepan. Cook over medium heat, stirring constantly, until smooth and creamy.

Variations

Toasted pound cake with ice cream and caramel sauce. Add sliced fresh peaches, bananas, or pecans, if you like.

Banana caramel sundaes with vanilla ice cream, caramel sauce, sliced bananas, and toasted nuts.

Turtle brownie sundaes with ice cream and caramel sauce.

Vanilla ice cream with caramel sauce topped with bits of crystallized ginger.

Stir a couple tablespoons of spiced rum, bourbon, Tennessee whiskey, or Scotch whisky into the sauce and serve over ice cream.

Toasted Marshmallow Sauce

There's no easier way to toast a marshmallow than by cheating with bottled smoke. This recipe takes a jar of old-school marshmallow cream blended with heavy cream, real vanilla, and smoke to make a modern miracle. Use it as you would any vanilla sauce with fresh fruits or berries, over ice cream, or in tandem with our cheater chocolate and caramel smoked dessert sauces.

MAKES 1 CUP

$1/2$ cup heavy cream

One 7- or $7^1/2$-ounce jar
   marshmallow cream

1 teaspoon vanilla extract

$1/2$ teaspoon bottled smoke

BRING the cream to a boil in a small saucepan over medium-high heat.

REDUCE the heat and stir in the marshmallow cream until smooth.

REMOVE from the heat and stir in the vanilla and bottled smoke. Serve warm or at room temperature.

A Big Pan of One-Pot Brownies

Homemade brownies are a good reminder that easy baking doesn't always involve a packaged mix or an electric mixer. These brownies require only a saucepan for melting the butter and chocolate. Once that's taken care of, stir in the rest of the ingredients and the batter is ready. That's it. The texture of these falls in the middle between the dense fudgy style and taller, cakier brownies. Min always takes her mother's advice and sprinkles the nuts on top so they'll toast in the oven.

A big pan of brownies can do anything. Pass a platter after a casual barbecue blow-out or dress them up with any or all three of the cheater smoked dessert sauces (pages 197 to 199) and ice cream.

MAKES 24 TO 36 BARS

- 12 tablespoons (1½ sticks) butter
- 6 ounces unsweetened chocolate, chopped
- 2 cups sugar
- 1½ cups self-rising flour
- 4 large eggs, beaten
- 2 teaspoons vanilla extract
- 1 teaspoon bottled smoke (optional)
- 1 cup chopped nuts (whatever kind you like—pecans, walnuts, almonds, pistachios, macadamias)

HEAT the oven to 350°F. Grease a 9 x 13-inch baking pan.

MELT the butter in a medium saucepan over low heat. Add the chocolate, stirring until melted.

REMOVE the pan from the heat and stir in the sugar, flour, eggs, vanilla, and bottled smoke, if using.

POUR the batter into the pan. Sprinkle the top with the nuts.

BAKE for 25 to 28 minutes, until the sides just begin to pull away from the pan. The center will seem set, but soft. Let the brownies cool in the pan on a rack for about 1 hour. Cut into bars.

Muffin-Cup Shortcake

Muffin-cup shortcakes made with self-rising flour turn shortcake biscuits into fast stir-up muffins. The muffins retain the biscuit qualities essential for shortcake—a crisp outer crust and a soft pillowy center that can hold up to a drenching of sweet fruit. Min sprinkles the muffin tops with fancy coarse sugar before baking because it looks pastry chef cool and has a nice crunch.

Strawberries are traditional and terrific, of course, but not the only fruit to use. We spoon on any fruit that's affordable, looks great, and is in season. Any berries or mix of berries and peaches are our summer favorites. In the winter we've made shortcake with sliced bananas, Smoky Caramel Sauce (page 198), and whipped cream.

MAKES 6 LARGE OR 12 SMALL SERVINGS

2 cups self-rising flour

1/4 cup granulated sugar

8 tablespoons (1 stick) butter, melted

1 cup milk

2 tablespoons coarse sugar (regular sugar also works fine)

Fresh fruits and berries such as blueberries, blackberries, sliced peaches, and nectarines, sweetened to taste (for 12 servings you'll need a good 6 to 8 cups of fruit)

Whipped cream

HEAT the oven to 450°F. Grease 12 muffin cups.

COMBINE the flour and granulated sugar in a medium mixing bowl. Stir in the butter and milk just until the dough is combined, but still slightly lumpy.

SPOON the dough evenly into the muffin cups; they'll be about half full. Sprinkle the tops with the coarse sugar.

BAKE for 12 to 15 minutes, or until the tops are golden brown and crisp. Cool slightly and remove from the muffin cups.

To serve, **SPLIT** the shortcakes, spoon the sweetened fruit over the halves, and top with whipped cream.

Swanky Figs

When our late summer/fall cheater barbecue party guests deserve something fancier than sliced watermelon, we serve *Swanky Figs*.

Like a good barbecue sauce, this dessert demonstrates the appeal of yin/yang balance—salty sharp blue cheese, creamy rich mascarpone, sweet honey, and tannic toasty walnuts. Go ahead and broil the figs early in the day. After dinner, discreetly step into the kitchen and reappear minutes later with a drop-dead platter of edible jewels.

MAKES 6 SERVINGS

6 fresh figs, cut in half

About 1 tablespoon olive oil

$^1/_2$ cup mascarpone cheese

3 ounces Stilton cheese (or any blue cheese), crumbled

$^1/_3$ cup walnut halves, toasted

About $^1/_4$ cup honey

HEAT the broiler.

PLACE the figs on a baking sheet and brush them lightly with the oil. Broil 4 inches from the heat source until lightly charred and softened, about 3 minutes per side.

SET the figs aside to cool at room temperature until serving time.

PLACE the figs on your nicest platter. Dollop each with a spoonful of mascarpone. Sprinkle each with some Stilton and walnuts. Drizzle with honey.

Broiled Peaches

Charred with butter and sugar, Broiled Peaches are a summertime romantic dinner-for-two essential in R. B.'s little black cookbook. Guys who lack strong dessert skills can relax. Broil the peaches early, set them aside at room temp, and assemble the dessert when ready to serve. R. B. likes his peaches with a scoop of vanilla ice cream, a splash of Amaretto, Smoky Caramel Sauce (page 198), and toasted sliced almonds on top.

Substitute fruits abound for this dish—you can butter, sugar, and broil banana halves, fresh pineapple spears, seeded melon wedges, and pitted and halved plums. We use whatever is in season. They all taste great with any of our cheater smoked dessert sauces.

MAKES 4 SERVINGS

2 ripe freestone peaches

3 tablespoons butter, melted

3 tablespoons brown sugar

Ice cream, liqueur, whipped cream, and/or chopped toasted nuts.

HEAT the broiler.

CUT the peaches in half and remove the pit. Place the peaches cut side down in a 9 X 13-inch baking pan.

BROIL 4 inches from the heat source for about 3 minutes, until lightly charred. Remove the peaches from the oven and turn them over, cut side up.

COMBINE the butter and sugar in a small bowl. Spread the mixture evenly over the peaches. Return to the oven and broil for 5 minutes, until bubbly and browned.

SERVE immediately or at room temperature with your choice of toppings.

Variations

Ice cream and sorbet flavors—butter pecan, raspberry sorbet, or peach on peach.

Sweet liqueurs—amaretto, framboise, hazelnut, and cassis.

Toppings—cheater smoked dessert sauces, whipped cream, mascarpone cheese, honey, crème fraîche, crumbled amaretti cookies, toffee bits, crumbled gingersnaps, granola, toasted pecans, almonds, macadamias, and pistachios.

Acknowledgments

We have many to thank for helping us along the way to barbecue freedom. Sincere thanks to our supportive agent, Mary Beth Chappell, who picked up the scent of good barbecue via e-mail. We are deeply grateful for the crack *Cheater BBQ* squad at Broadway Books, who we hope can each claim a large slow cooker by now—our editor, Jennifer Josephy, and her right hand, Stephanie Bowen; production editor, Ada Yonenaka; designer, Elizabeth Rendfleisch; marketing manager, Julie Sills; and copyeditor, Sarah Weaver.

Thanks also to our dear friend and colleague Anne Byrn, for years of great fun, food, and encouragement; to Al Matteson and Mr. James Harvey of Fixed Rite Repair in Charlestown, Rhode Island, for flaming up the slow cooker and R. B.'s 1969 Honda CL450; and to our multitalented Cheater Chef team in Nashville, designer Bob Delevante of Relay Station and Web designer Tamra Stallings.

We cherish our friends and families for their unconditional love and support, especially our kitchen-table taste-testers, Louis Dunn and Elsa Dunn.

R. B. Quinn and Mindy Merrell
Nashville, Tennessee

Index

INDEX

INDEX

About the Authors

Mindy Merrell and R. B. Quinn cook, eat, and write in Nashville, Tennessee. After years of splitting wood, endless fiddling with smoker vents, and stirring up secret sauces, they've grown to appreciate the convenience of all-natural liquid smoke in a regular kitchen, and a good night's sleep. They are dedicated champions of barbecue diversity, from the open pit to the closed oven and slow cooker. Visit them at www.cheaterchef.com.